Iota

89

Iota 89

Contacting Iota

Website: www.iotamagazine.co.uk
Editor: editor@iotamagazine.co.uk
Features: features@iotamagzine.co.uk
Listings: listings@iotamagazine.co.uk
Subscriptions: subs@iotamagazine.co.uk

Please send all correspondence and submissions to:
Iota
PO Box 7721
Matlock
DE4 9DD

Iota 89
ISBN 978-1-906285-89-0
ISSN 0266-2922 £6.50

Design & Layout:
Raphael Tassini & Andrea De Cal
Printed & Bound in India
Cover Image: Courtesy private collection

www.iotamagazine.co.uk

Contents

Editorial Spring 2011

The editorial team welcome you to another issue of Iota. We are very pleased with it, and we hope you will be too. There are a wide variety of styles represented from across the UK and Ireland and one or two from further afield. Among the contributors to this issue we are delighted to include David Holliday, the founder of the journal.

Auden famously wrote 'poetry makes nothing happen' and David Morley has said 'poetry is the opposite of money'. So why do we do it? Why do we obsess over a word or a line, spend hours getting a few words in the right order, and give all our time and energy to this 'sullen art' which will neither earn us enough to live on nor make anything happen? Perhaps because we believe poetry matters.

Millions of people reach for poetry at times of crisis, either reading it or writing it, and while we may scorn the easy sentimentality of much of the poetry written and read at such times, it clearly meets a need. Poetry can connect with those things for which we have no words, can say the un-sayable and, I think most importantly, explain ourselves to ourselves. There are thousands of quotes, attempts to define what poetry is, or what it does, and there are so many because no single definition can garner universal agreement. Poetry may connect with what is un-sayable but what it is, and does, is also apparently something for which we have no words; so we reach for metaphor: *Poetry is the journal of the sea animal living on land, wanting to fly in the air.* (Sandburg); *Poetry is boned with ideas, nerved and blooded with emotions, all held together by the delicate, tough skin of words* (Engle); *Imaginary gardens with real toads in them* (Moore).

Poetry matters. There are some who would say that only the poetry found in the pages of magazines like this one, or between the covers of a slim volume, is the poetry that matters. There are others who would say that only performance poetry matters, or page poetry, or post-avant, or experimental, or formalist, or mainstream. There are those who believe that poetry is somehow weakened or contaminated by the ease of publishing on the internet and others who think that university creative writing courses are sequestering poetry behind academic barriers. Such divisions are pointless and largely a waste of creative energy because it all matters. From a child's first experience of poetry in nursery rhymes, to cozy writing groups, to a teenager's cliché-ridden online diary entry, to open mics, to journal publication, prizes and awards; everyone engages with poetry in the way that suits them, to suit an individual need and in doing so finds a way of expressing what is essentially human, for the arts and creativity are what makes us human.

Most of the poetry being written, or spoken, isn't publishable by the usual standards of others wanting to read it, nor would most poetry being written garner critical acclaim but then no-one expects that everyone who picks up a camera will exhibit at *Paris Photo*; that doesn't mean that the poems, or photos, are entirely without value. If we believe poetry matters, then it all matters because it all contributes to keeping poetry alive, changing and developing. It would be fatal to regard poetry as worthwhile only if it achieves critical acclaim. It would soon be elitist, sterile - and dead.

All the arts matter, if creativity is what makes us human, and poetry is a minority interest in the arts. In these days of cuts and austerity, when arts organisations of all sizes are seeing their grant funding cut and statutory funding is being withdrawn from university arts and humanities courses, we are in danger of sleepwalking into a bleak Gradgrindian world where only utility and profitability is valued. Poetry, being such a small part of the arts, is in danger of being squeezed into invisibility unless those of us who think it matters stand up for it. Poetry doesn't need marches and protests though, it only needs commitment: subscribing to poetry journals, buying books from small (unfunded) presses, attending poetry readings and open mics. As long as there is an audience to read or listen, poetry is alive.

Angela France
Features Editor

Poetry

Mike Barlow

The Pall Bearers

(after 'The Journey' by Fenwick Lawson,
St Mary's Church, Lindisfarne)

Who is it they bear across the sand,
these six hewn faces set
                              to the polishing wind,
their long box lodged on elm shoulders,
the gouged flow of their habits?

Where are they coming from,
and where are they going, their journey
a dark mass moving
                              and not moving
through sea-fret?

Whose soul is it their load's the lighter for,
the weight of a lark's song lighter,
climbing beyond hearing?
And is it this we feel,
                              the lark's return,
a stone's weight of feather coming to rest
among thrift and pebbles again?

Whoever it is they bear towards us
the bearers step further away as we watch.
The sea alone
                    will nourish them,
their elm hearts given to the waves
to wash up in the tideline's debris,
broken and worked as beads.

Mike Barlow

Local History

Some nights the valley's a river of children.
I hear their invisible hopscotch and tag,
their movements shadowed by water,
its eddies, splashes, the all-of-a-sudden

silence a pool emits like a sigh.
There's the jump of a shout like a fish
or a secret spilled in a panic of giggles,
cross your heart and hope to die.

Or there's a shriek; it could be a game
or it could be the girl whose father
would, years later, shoot himself
for reasons her mother couldn't explain.

And the two boys fighting are my neighbour
and the milkman, who'll both end up
the best of mates. I hear
their grunts and thumps as they labour

away at some family grudge
neither understands. And those twin sisters
who emigrated years ago, they're paddling
about on a raft their father's bodged

from plastic barrels and a broken gate.
Yes, there are children here who'll carry
the valley with them like a faith;
and others the river still holds in their place.

I listen as voices leapfrog back upriver,
a weave of echoes called back home
where a gutter sings in the peat,
moorland rain trickles through heather.

Mike Barlow

Skull Spirit
(English Family China 1998, by Christine Borland, The Tate Gallery, Liverpool)

Bone chamber of my children's ghosts,
I should have found a settling place,
been left amongst the worms
not dug from the earth like a tuber,
polished and wrapped in cloth,
transported
over seas of strange ideas.

Now my bone china cast
sits carefully positioned
on a plate glass plinth,
a wreath of willow pattern
tattooed on my pate.

Visitors admire my glaze,
the clean set of my jaw,
the perfect row of teeth I have acquired
in the name of good taste;
in their minds take tea
and cucumber sandwiches,
imagine salt brown men
change rigs on clippered seas.

But when they peer into my sockets
it's then I long to make
the trade winds shift,
hear their words gag
on the stench of another cargo.

Displayed here in a bright white room,
I am inheritance
made safe by clever thoughts
scrubbing history clean.

The sign reads *Do Not Touch.*
I wait for someone one day
to have had enough,
pick up the nearest piece of china,
smash it on the wall,
set me free.

Retrospect

In my story, you walked to school that day,
left the moped in the garage with your
gauntlets on the seat, caught up with me,
suggested we should meet back at your house,
your brother still at work. I tell myself
we carry on from there, off and on
until I move away. Now say you're twenty-five
and have learnt the art of smiling. We talk
about that time you waited in the bath
next to your parents' kitchen after school.
But the story won't make sense, the facts
you left too small to be given consequence.
I can't put explanations in your mouth.
You just stand there in the kitchen doorway,
pencil slim and pale and carrying a helmet.

A Few Fields

He had a landscape in his head: neat fields
with sheep sculpting the light, chewing and stopping,
then moving on, measuring the distance
between the embankment pocked with rabbit holes,
the abandoned house and railway bridge.
And if it was a map inside his head,
instead of moving images – elm trees
leaning across a fence, shifting cows –
he could walk his fingers from bridge to bridge,
imagine nettles and the smell of wild garlic.
Each bridge would tell a different story: a crayfish
inside a plastic shoe; the place the dog
jumped in and barked and bit the water; the blur
of a kingfisher. He'd walk his fingers over
the iron bridge to where he took the boy,
where they'd hid and touched each other's groin,
or he'd walk them back along the brook, until
they came to where a chestnut-coloured horse
stood in the centre of a field of ice.

Reading Elizabeth Jennings

This is a good model; words that hold
across the page and can say
'rose' or 'river' seriously,
without disdain,

can take as subject frost or rain –
the taste of tea. My thoughts
(she helps me say it now) break in
and spoil it all:

the body that might fall
around itself, the breath finding
an old zinc bucket to rock itself in
and the lotus opening.

Giraffe

We have washed you
Demerara and blonde
in the English sun.
Your head, of
lantern complexity –
interstellar eyes

and exuberant lashes –
is a mask of lost time:
furred stump-horns
and a grey, snake-like
tongue that can
pick off the best.

One of your hooves
is twisted in the
scuffed-up straw.
Bending towards us,
like a rucked-up duvet
too big for its cover,

you take slice after
slice of brown bread
from your keeper,
who tells us
you are the oldest lady
in captivity,

a hybrid
that will not be bred.
You watch us with
departing eyes, your
ancient soul already
striding in the Serengeti.

White Coats

My eyes can't escape this room, can't crawl out
without being seen. I'm in lung-deep,
reeking of cigarettes, my x-ray looks like a night

window I could lunge through. It is me. I show up in its silence.
A snapshot negative.

My face stops, stares back in disbelief,
looks at itself with the curiosity of a stranger. Panic-stricken
I extend my hand ready for a firm shake.

Since that first day the machine bleeps rhythmically,
never missing a beat. The sheets are taut as a drum
around me and the hum of the lights goes on into the night.

Shift change. They all smell the same. They watch me
sleep and wake and sleep and wake,

wired up with no means of escape. Their voices like a radio
tuning in and out, sentences sucking themselves
from of this place.

                    My body has enough.
Disguised as a crow it flies from my mouth.
On the bed an egg, speckled blue, loses its warmth.

Iris

On the ledges of my eyes
flies knit their wings

and dream of their inheritance
in the shade of the lids.

They have nothing
on their minds but my mind.

Slipping their wings
over themselves, they burrow

into sockets, hind legs folding
as they hide in sticky hollows.

I blink unwillingly,
check my cheeks,

but their movement
hardly involves my face

Insomnia

I hear those whispers again,
ones which persist through the night.

I clap my hands to my head,
listen to the sea; it draws me back.

I follow you to the beach,
see your prints in the sand,

and step into them. They are too far apart.
I jump, sand caves in around my feet,

wind stings my eyes, hurls and
sings in my ears. I jam my fingers in,

soften the sound of the sea
and lose the outline of your shoes,

crouch, snatch the sand,
scratch it with my fingernails.

In the sea you are staring at me.
It called to you, quietly at first,

waking you to its idea, but later told you:
walk up to your neck and don't look back.

The Last Moment

Just before the end I run from the house
clutching the key in my left fist,
arms moving in wide loops.

I crack in two, break free from myself
and the part of me you want peels
from my grasp, accelerates down the street.

I watch my life pick up steam,
that self's a bee swarm, loud, thick –
a black buzz droning down the road.

I'm far behind at the pelican crossing
reeling on the kerb as bees spin, skim the sky,
their rage beating in their wings.

The green man beckons me to cross.
My slippers have darkened at the toe,
turned from pink to black and at the back

of my head I hear you shouting,
doors slamming, and know the tracks
of my feet lead back to you.

I want to come home to stillness,
a slept-in-late feeling, wake to a muttering day.
But I sprint, slippers skidding

trying to catch myself before I disappear from view.

Koi

Not one to complain, not one to make herself felt,
she could, without prompting, hold her breath

and glide from one end of the pool to the other,
through the silent water, in her orange bathing suit.

She wouldn't complain about the bikini I bought her,
she just didn't wear it – too many eyes, too much flesh –

so bending back, like a goodbye hand waving to herself,
she appears a glowing encarpus hidden inside her depth.

On The Terrace

Voices from the pool, the glad-to-be-dead people, echo off the tiles
escorting the living beyond the cars to the beach sloping under the wreck
and tideline and away into the chemical arms of truth and love.
We likewise could have been here forever, drinking Guinness halves
and sweet Illy coffee on the terrace in the same silence we keep for hours
totally our own: not angry, just concerned there is nothing left
to talk about; nothing left to share. Clouds trawl the bay, and the fleet
of soul-white rocks in the noon light, just as we are a bit iffy, queasy,
squinting into the glare, hot and on the shakiest of grounds, sand
or sediment, and I'm still quiet when we get home and it's too late
to say anything at all... On the balcony above, not even trying
to stay out of earshot, twin-suited businessmen, fat and thin, debate
the server in Sweden, sub-reflective particles and telecom solutions.
They call Dublin and Leeanne is soon on the case. She will ring them back.

Occasional Traffic

In no time Krazy Kabs ring back on your trim mobile,
the thrill of a blackbird inside your bag. It's a technical advance,
and intrusive, making you rush to put yourself together,
as if being watched. The air is colder for being closer to dawn,
your other life about an hour away through the gaps
in occasional traffic and the streetlights going out...
You may have all your clothes or he may have the rest,
nevertheless you are heading home alone, an orphan prodigal
tarting up eyes and lips, fixing seams and creases,
and leaving the door wide-open for that bye-bye smile.
You won't worry until morning – morning almost upon you;
worry in the sense that no trace of you will remain
except the flavour of this parting, and that something
of the replay will come back to haunt you with a vengeance.

Suburban

Replete with 'A' level mothers on nicotine,
the untrendy student musicheads, their elbows
squeezing archfiles of encrypted statistics
or microbiology notes, new hieroglyphs for
the electrical engineer, or more seriously
the runes of sex, drugs and how many drinks,
or last night's box from the pose of a cynic,

they take the suburban service over brittle
sleepers losing out to the frost, the slow train
on a long descent between yards and depots,
past difficult back-to-back outskirts, cursory
speed-ramps and someone's idea of a hospital,
to an itsy-bitsy platform held together
by the language of the id in broad felt-tip.

Prussia Cove

On black rocks my foot slips, we shudder
and taste the salt drip on our tongues,
sway like drunks in the night. My lungs
could crack with cold. This is the place

I wanted to see but now, under the flat
gaze of molluscs we are stripped open
by rain, your form darkens and drifts
leeward in a tangle of rope and kelp.

I picture tea chests, spilled sacks, decks
yawing with pewter, plate, the gold coins
of someone's fortune sent elsewhere
but destined for this beach. The wives

held the lanterns, it's said, and I see them:
high up on the cliff, as wind stones their faces,
wet shawls whip shut their eyes, up there
where herring gulls caw their warning.

Robin Houghton

I was once the Pope

This is not what I expected.
Red was my colour, or white,
white as a virgin's skin. Robes
hung from me as delicate
as the smooth charcoal tissue
that floats from the fire.

Each year I am reincarnate.
Children press their fingers
to my frame, glue and paper
swaddling these new bones
of wood and chicken wire.
In six months I am fleshed.

My face grows more grotesque
with the passing years, ears
larger, cheeks greyer. Knock
your knuckle on my body
and hear my hollowness.
But I am not without substance:

I am laced with the stuff of death.
At first, the heat agonised me.
Now I welcome it, I am ready.
Red is my colour – red as earth
scorched through and bloodied
red as a child's gaudy toy.

And when this shell explodes,
splinters of me will grate the sky,
the crowd will be sated.
You can look for me if you must –
trodden into mud, dusting trees –
go on, stare. I am not there.

The Ordeal

A man now,
he thinks back to the ordeal

of the consecration of the host,
the agony as a boy

of kneeling and waiting,
the suffering from bell to bell,

so short a time but he remembers
only waste and pain,

and the way summer hit him
as he stepped out

after mass and was free, driven home
and off to find the other boys

playing,
rolling an enormous emptied wooden cable spool

down the field's slow incline,
in the heat, in the insect-swim, running and goading the spool

which was twice as tall as the tallest of them
into a deadly kind of life,

a machine of pure unnecessity,
a monstrous flywheel of joy.

The Landlord at North Pond

When summer comes with its bags of sugar
and newlyweds tickle the pond,
naked
among the milfoil,

he never fails to reach for his smock
to find an old lemon,
bruised
and aching for the knife.

At Whately Diner

The hairs on Audrey's legs were as long as her eyelashes, which were very long, forming a dark corona around her irises. Her irises possessed the soft, bruised color of old lettuce, a greeny brown which was the same greeny brown as the section of wallpaper in her bathroom which she'd wanted to replace since moving last January. The rest of the bathroom was either tiled or papered the color of the flesh of her eyes, or of the blurt of semen which three years from now would get her pregnant, or of cauliflower. Using her own hands, which possessed the soft, bruised texture of old lettuce, she might have afforded to repaper her bathroom on the living she made serving chicken pie the color of her unpainted nails and strawberry-rhubarb pie the color of the rim of her nostrils, but the time was never there. Her hands and her nails and her nostrils were as they were because she had spent yesterday on her knees in her mother's flower garden, turning soil and gathering up year-old leaves and stalks which grotesquely resembled the soup of leftovers described on the chalkboard today as "vegetable soup." Her handwriting on the chalkboard resembled her mother's handwriting on a birthday card she got last month with two sets of earrings and a daily planner in which weeks-at-a-glance alternated with photographs of Renaissance sculpture. The eyes of those naked marble figures had the shape but not the color of her own eyes the way cauliflower had the shape but not the color of broccoli. Those marble heads with their marble hair themselves resembled cauliflower, though not the cauliflower used in the "vegetable soup," which at that point was coming apart the way the year-old leaves were coming apart into soil, or the way she was coming apart into her mother. After the gardening she helped her mother to make broccoli soup, and the soup smelled like fennel, which smelled like tarragon, which smelled like aniseed. The color of the soup was the unlikely avocado color of the tabletops at a restaurant where she would dine with the man whose semen would get her pregnant three years from now. His irises would be the color of the soil she turned yesterday in her mother's garden, and the piece of strawberry-rhubarb pie she would share with him would have flesh the color of the flesh she would share with him later that night.

She wrung a rag and made everything as new as she could.

In the map gaps

By the time I reach the mobile
the caller's hung up. I stare
at the missed call number,
willing it to form a pattern
I might recognise. I don't
return the call, in case it's someone
from one of those mythical kingdoms –
West Anglia, North Saxonland,
the South Riding of Yorkshire.

Some nights the wind comes
from a direction that doesn't exist,
and there are voices in it
that I know are crying.

Leaving the nests

Ant tunnels fill with excitement
and pheromones. Fat
winged alates jostle past
sexless workers, fighters,
boil out of the entrance, take off
for their nuptial flight.

In the sky silent gulls
fly open-mouthed
through the swarms,
jinking, dipping, tumbling,
taking their formic harvest,
a pungent feast. Those missed
pair in the air, fall to ground,
shed once-used wings. Males die,
but fertilised queens crawl off
to found new empires.

Land

My vegetable patch is six feet square.
Dandelions and ragwort are rowdy
on the sidelines, but the bean plants slip
shy tendrils around their canes
and dance, awkward partners, in the wind.

I've become my own scarecrow. When I work
straw hair hangs down uncut.
I've a rifle in a drawer, a bicycle,
five nearly-new blankets. Come evening
I will wear one like a cloak and light a fire.

All night the gutter chatters itself loose.
Tomorrow I'll get up at dawn and wire it tight.
I'll climb to the top of the rusting caravan
and look towards the sea. Everything
between here and the sand dunes is mine.

Silfra

Galvanise yourself. Rubbery as a seal, androgynous
and wetsuit-sticky. It will pinch every hair on you.

The water here is glass clear, so cold
it almost chimes with ice. You capsize

into the seam between two continents
that edge around each other, facing, tentative.

Will they, won't they? Ask the other one
to dance, or to help them start a war.

They shuffle apart by millimetres. In the towns
they make their churches of corrugated steel.
The airports have been closed for weeks.

Telephone

Alexander's brothers died at a young age.
The three of them had made a pact –
Whoever was left would invent a machine
and learn to converse with the dead.

The dial of the telephone chattered
like unearthed bones, and chimed
like a graveyard on a windy night.

Perhaps at first he thought the voice
was a lost sibling, words creeping up
the dark coil, into his ear
between lips as cold as bakelite.

Three Books About Cats

Brought up so well to respect my betters,
tall ladies with long teeth, my teacher,
the barber, the rector with his surgical boot,
Miss Gaffney next door
who worked in the laundry
and every book that came into my hands,
I stooped to pick up three square, yellow hardbacks
of Would-You-Believe-It? yarns about cats
that I'd knocked with my jacket off the rack
alongside the queue in Waterstone's.
The woman I almost bumped into behind me
(who wasn't irritated or impatient
and gave no hint of her feelings for cats)
stepped back and said with a terse kindliness
as I ran my fingers along the rack
to find the pile they'd fallen from,
For Christ's sake, just leave them.
Just leave them. Don't worry.

Robert Etty

Sleep Unsound

Sleep's a gossamer thing for over-fifties ...
- Richard Ford 'The Lay of the Land'

You turn the bedroom lights out one by one.
Financial news comes on the radio. Two football scores.
The body found near Swindon might be who they think.
In half an hour, tomorrow's weather's going to be today's.
Darkness lightens. Furniture defines its selves.
You click the radio off and see the red dot go.
You're turning over, pedalling, readjusting pillows
and the quilt you want around your ears, and then you don't.
You find the same position as last night's, the one
that takes the pressure off the pressure points,
and listen to your breathing drawing deep and slowing down.
Sleep should wash over soon, providing that you haven't
eaten after nine, drunk coffee, catnapped,
lost control (or keys), or heard surprising news,
and that tomorrow you're not starting something,
ending it, expecting trouble, flying,
seeing someone who'll upset your applecart
or entertaining the unentertaining.
Sleep saturates. For now, it's all there is.
But, even in unconsciousness, you'll sense what's going
to wake you up before it does: cars, barks, the floorboard
that you never hear in daytime groaning.
A night-noise or, sometimes, a freeze-framed dream
will crash through your film of sleep and tip you
back on your bed in a room in the house you'll be
leaving after you've turned over, pedalled, fluffed up
your pillows and made yourself think about
anything other than lying there thinking of sleep:
verses of songs you'd forgotten till now;
lists of favourite foods, or the fortunate sweethearts
you didn't marry; registrations of cars you drove.
Images pass like crows flapping over a field.
You drift to a beach, a road, Paris in rain,

the Boulevard de Courcelles, past the peach stalls, patisserie,
red-doored tabac where you fumble with euros,
and never remember which is the image that leads you
to where your alarm's tired of biting its tongue.
Before long, you've taken the morning in hand
and your seek-and-hide games with gossamer sleep
were insomniac dreams with dawn chorusing through.
As you're driving home, lampposts repeat themselves
and wet tyres swoosh past your halfway-down window.
Your car seat begins to wrap round like a quilt and
it's almost as if you could stretch your whole length,
switch the radio off, be still, and sleep.

The Duck Pond At Etton

It was ten past three by my watch, dead on,
when the red roofs of Etton rose over treetops
blown back in the straight-across wind.
Brian pulled his glove off and hooked back his sleeve.
“It’s just gone five to nine,” he said.
“If I wind this watch, you know, it stops.
If I twist my wrist, it starts again,
but I didn’t twist my wrist today.”
We sat at the duck pond at twenty past
on a Jubilee bench with its legs bolted down.
A woman shopping called when she saw us,
“Don’t look for ducks on that blinking duck pond!
Somebody’s culled the blinking lot!”
At half-past, nearly, as long-tailed tits flitted
where unculled ducks should be waddling and paddling,
we synchronised our standing up
and set off for Scorborough side by side
and six hours and several minutes apart.

Copse

The night before the night before the wedding.
Cut the ignition, let the car roll in neutral

the last few feet aside that *shock* of crow-rattled
trees. You've been riding the lanes with these women all week,

their backs arching eternally to gasps and pouts
of simulated pleasure, muffled in straining bin-liners,

misting black plastic. Your memory is scarred
by after-images of epilated bodies, splayed

for the camera's glassy eye— ghosts burned
in the screen of a superseded arcade console.

You un-clunk the boot with unusual care, feel
the weight of the magazines sag in your fist, livid

angles piercing the surface. A half-run
through slick grass—your under-arm lob sends a pheasant

blundering through thicket, its idiot squawk races
the pulses of village boys who spill your bachelor

secret, turn the sheen of its pages. Mouths
dry. Ears hot. They tense at any

creak or snap announcing whatever it is
that too soon bears down upon them.

Symphony of Horror

That was the summer I thought we'd die pretty soon.
Tanks rolled in cheaply improvised republics
and scientists deep in the earth banged bits of Creation
together, like happy toddlers. In the suburbs,

I couldn't sleep. Machinery chewed up the night—
the sound of the edges of everything fraying to nothing,
or missiles tying the earth in ribbons of after-burn.
I imagined our embrace glowing like a wick

in human grease. Death had me hypnotised.
I almost loved him. So, he did whatever
he wanted, never asked me for my safe word.

In my chamber, I watched him glide towards me,
a fanged phallus, smothering me with his silhouette.
No point in my betrothed screaming in montage,

when this is what I really want.

Lizard

That summer was slimy-hot; the air a damp broth
Even under a ceiling made for acrobats

One afternoon, my skin greased from the fan's brew
I saw a lizard flash along the wainscot

A minnow of dark light; a film of displaced dust
Thin as the skin between laughter and tears

Weeks later, I woke at dawn to scuffling
Curious, foreign, Polanski-sinister

I lay there waiting for the wall to crack
Curtains to buckle in an absent wind

While the lizard said farewell
And the first chord of autumn blew in from the sea

For Isabella

I wake to fear and a froth of birdsong
The curtains swollen with underwater light
The canal taut as a layer of cellophane

A painter sends me lines she has written
In a language that I do not speak
Knowing I have the root to hand

Certain words reveal themselves like flowers
Others clasp their provenance bud-tight
I map a course across the Mediterranean

Out-running my own demons in pursuit
Of another woman's fantasy
As the sky thickens, poised for thunder

For Francesca Woodman

(after Adrienne Rich)

The fact of a doorframe
gave you something to hold on to

as you moved through the world skinless
wearing your broken rooms like water

you propped Euclid on your pillow
turned your lens on his mute glass eyes

finding infinity in fugitive corners
pockets of grace in imprecise angles

prowling those parched thresholds
like a cat seeking sunlight

less narcissist than pilgrim child
undressing the elements like dolls

Corte Sconta

Our hands clasped across the table.
A prayer of fingers; text of flesh.

Wrestling need out of the mute oak.
It could be Paris, Dakar, ancient Rome.

We have built a pyramid of blame.
Stacking fault with the precision of children.

The waiters drop their charm offensive.
The rose seller gives us a wide berth.

Certain of victory, Language slinks off.
Our world cropped to the theatre of cutlery.

And you take my hand. Silence ruptures.
A couple close to us start to quarrel.

Fess Parker Is Dead

Kilt him a b'ar when he was only three.
-"Davy Crockett, King of the Wild Frontier"

Jesus, you could practically mark the full-
on blast-off of American marketing
from the craze for all those plastic powder
horns and trading cards, the coloring books
and lunch boxes and half a million

coonskin caps on the crewcut heads of boys
in every suburban yard from Binghamton
to Hermosa Beach. Alas, television
is a fickle deity and nylon fringe
wears out fast: Davy Crockett and Daniel Boone

retired from the wilds of Tennessee to distant
Santa Barbara, opened a winery
and resort. Everyone I know here
disliked him. Pigheaded, they said, mad
to develop every inch of open land,

always on the lookout for a buck—
though you heard, too, he was soft-spoken,
courtly even as he ground you down.
And I had a fondness for his '06 Syrah.
My wife and I stayed once at his Inn

and Spa in Los Olivos—overpriced
with a lousy view, but the fireplace
was nice. I never met him; now he's gone.
"Natural causes," the family reports,
as though there were any other kind.

David Starkey

To the Homeless of Santa Barbara

The world does not look kindly
  On poverty and anguish:
Filthy women and spindly-
  Legged men, drunk in cloddish,
Cast-off Clothing, each ripped apart
Life trundled in a shopping cart,
      Bedsore,
      Eyesore
Impossible to ignore.

And yet somehow we manage
  To make you briefly vanish
As we walk past your wreckage,
  Snubbing what we would banish.
It's just you make such a racket
As you whiskey and six-pack it
      Toward
      Discord
And the bliss of not being bored.

What in the world can we do
  For you who seem so careless
Of life's niceties? Rescue?
  A stab at friendship? Largesse?
Your heavy loss at life's roulette
Makes you so easy to forget.
      Shalom.
      At home
I barely think to write this poem.

The Laughter of Women

Five minutes from the home of Stockport County. Tannoy words
blur around the edges, apologies for the late running of this train. Small birds
are swirling in the air above a sleep-in of sheep. I love the way they work the light,
inside out, upside down, as if they're threading seeds in furrows of air
and in a sudden switch of blades, put the valley on its feet. Today,
we will meet in a café with a beautiful name. We'll bounce like loose limes
down a walnut stairway that opens on grained-pine tables and benches.
Spoons and forks will be made of bamboo or bonsai, as will the black-pepper pot
that will remind me of a rolling pin. I'll take off my watch, shoes, clothes;
you will smile. I'll put them back on again. We will eat black-eyed bean pie
and an orange served on a saucer; segments spooning in two symmetrical lines.
You will rearrange the bones in my right hand. I will feel as serene as a buddha's cat
on St Kilda. Your eyes will bring to mind a peacock-blue freshwater lake
skimmed with mist. The glittering turquoise splash of a kingfisher.
In Oxford Road station, I am walking towards the laughter of women.

Steve Sawyer

Unlike the Sun

You, perched like a herring gull's breast on top of the Woodseats Friary
and at noon. Sun cold, the day. I think of how many words you unwrite
as they are being written (without prejudice, I like to think).
Words that compare you to a golden cream palomino thoroughbred
or a bucket of frozen tripe. All the false-starts, indecisions, revisions:
sixty a day for Joan of Flashbacks, eating pickled onions
in the Three Boys Café. Shall I find you compared to a butternut
on her serviette? Here on earth the usual; glad dogs, tail-lights, postcards.
Journeys: rubbery mouthed pensioners eating cod en route from the chip shop
to the chemist. All the early arrivals, late departures, one and the same.
How you pull the strings unnoticed, abandon yourself unbeaten
wearing silk pyjamas. How slight the difference between a body of words
that earns its place with poems and a plastic moon tied to a wooden horse
on a gilded carousel. I read of the Forth Bridge painter who no longer knows
where he ends and the bridge begins. See a Great Dane flexi-lead lengthening,
bring the owner up short in a wrap-around at the traffic lights.
Look for the page on which you are compared to a tangle of trout.

Classically Trained

He's been seen wearing exquisite rags from the Lost and Found,
a kettle of leaves and mumbles. He once wore an Elvis suit
at an embassy dinner. Medicated courtesans were flown in
by *Jet Star*. 'Blueberry', the depressed ballerina
from the New York Met. That Thai masseuse they found dead
in the Paris Hilton: his private number like stigmata on her tan.
Oh, he has the people's blood on his sundial, for sure.
Those intelligence dossiers in western sideboards,
next to crosswords and jigsaws. He's as guilty as old Salah.
After all, there's no smoke without ballistic missile systems.

In the beginning he tackled the shortfall in camels and dreams.
Kissed ten babies, put out the sun. Restored the fish supper
and typewriter. No end of fun was to be had in the tea rooms.
Then his ideas began to explode in the high streets and tramcars.
People bled in the barbers. Surgeons ran out of arms and legs.
Horses lay like broken saddles on the edge of smoking cities.
No one could find the weapons of mass amnesia.
I'm the same with theatre tickets when the play is weeks away.
He forgot where he'd left them. Remember the days of triumph?
He wore the People's thin cotton black pyjama garb.
His moustache was a panther's silence. His stallion, a silhouette.
He said politics is the minted breath of a patron saint,
a hand that holds a fountain pen. Walmart in Madagascar,
star-spangled hunger. He was never known to kill anyone
with a good supply of fingernails. A rice field worker
saw him reading Homer in a rickshaw as enemy tanks
knocked down the gates. The press said it was one of the doubles.
They employ 26 classically-trained actors. It's the only role
they play. He's a difficult man to sum up.

When I saw him he looked like a man pouring tea from a flask
in the foreshock of footlights, as he waited for the din to die down.

Common Language

Arc, he says.

She sees several animals
ill at ease with each other,
bobbing on boards above water.

He means fire and air -
science-words, precise:
the spark that jumps the gap.

Now she sees words coming to land
elbowing up to be first off
loaded like donkeys at a fair.

They tinkle and clang like pot lids
hesitate, stutter, taste strange air -
then jump the gap.

Metaphor

for my sister

D'you remember –
when grown-ups sang about flames of love
and you imagined real fire inside their chest?

and legs turning to jelly
were wobble-columns
razzle-red and lemon yellow?

and glassy-eyed
was marbles rolling
bony-clank down cheeks?

and metaphor
was the hardest thing
the teacher ever had to teach?

Now look at us.

We're bags-for-life,
leaving ourselves on a park bench

we're trees, defoliate
there, on the lower limbs
and in the under-branch pits
and in that private place
where the limbs fork.

Oh my dear –
our bits are in free-fall

our metaphors so mixed, so rich
the edges blur

we could be anything.

Pam Brough

Worlds Apart

A woman is pulling up onions
in a garden just behind the cliff edge.

Something comes between
herself and her hands.

Somewhere –
possibly along the beach below -
a thin strip is being torn
from the surface of the world.

The woman thinks of a small man
riding a bicycle,
his head bobbing with effort

the wheels lifting and winding up
this thin line of land
which will eventually pass right round the world
and slice it in half.

She cannot hear
the creak of the wheel as it turns,
but something is pushing the edges of her day
into a small circle.

She carries on pulling up onions.
The world being the way it is,
this is all she can do.

Someone is watching her.
Another makes small electronic notes.

She slips the wet skin from each bulb,
the wet brown outer skin
that slides down and gets stuck
in the top of the roots,
where the black soil clings.

They want to know why.
She could say
it is only a sense of not-right,
of possible decay.

She would also need to say
it is the onion, sitting in the hand,
instructs the fingers
what to take, what to leave alone.

There is too much to tell,
so she says nothing.

It is so far back,
it is someone else's fingers
working through her own.

But she can foresee a day
when her unsaid words
will be brought together
under their name.

It will be a very straight day,
with defined edges.

There will be no cacaphony of distraction
no beetle on his back, pedalling air,
no gravelled worm on the path,
no bright, beguiling presence of the sea.
It will be very efficient.

Their voices drop like plums.
She cannot leave them
lying on the grass.
There must be some exchange.

But they have moved on.
They are somewhere just out of sight –
perhaps on the beach
following a thin line in the sand,

taking away a glory, or at least
a small bright difference,
leaving a shadow on the ground.

Jonathan Taylor

D.P.I.

He is pixellated
when I zoom
into memories,

magnifying,
blurrifying
low-res grains,

as if,
technologically,
1980s neurons are
1980s silicone.

The past is all
jagged lines,

and, closer,
a hazy helicopter tie
in diagonal
            block graphics
                        is upwards-leading,
            to the reverse stairways
of his collar,

and, closer still,
I am one of the squares,

lost in Escherian geometries.

Joy

After Oliver Sacks, Musicophilia, *chapter 6*

At sixty, she woke into a non-stop *Ode to Joy*,
and couldn't switch off these L.P.-ish hallucinations,
playing at the wrong r.p.m.s, squeaking like a toy,
or yawningly slow, tired from incessant celebrations.

Beethoven stalked her, like Pink Panther's cloud,
to Post Office, hairdresser's, on the phone,
her nerve-deafness, once so quiet, now loud,
filled with *O Freunde, nicht diese Töne!*

G.P.s and consultants gave her E.E.G.s, M.R.I.s,
showing blossomings in the basal ganglia,
up to the thalamocortical systems, musical lies
scored for chorus and full orchestra.

They put her on gabapentin, risperidone,
checked for cerebral aneurysms,
gave her quetiapine, prednisone,
an analyst tried therapy for narcissism,

but nothing worked, and she felt stampeded
by pressing Brotherhood, drunk from Nature's wine,
recitatived, *presto*ed and *allergro energico*ed
into submission, and marched into line.

Forced to ear-drink at the *Brüsten der Natur*,
she unremembered nursing long-ago
as a young girl: "You're so mature,"
they'd said, but life had never felt so slow

before or after, when she'd tried returning
to college and its choir – no longer wanted:
"You'll need time for grieving, not learning,"
they'd said, meaning: forget life, get husbanded,

have another. But she'd thought she hadn't
liked the first, till too late, Beethoven-haunted,
Joy's timpani seemed more like a mallet,
the trumpets, like tannoys, feedback-distorted;

and, as time went on, the ear assaults shortened,
no longer whole recitatives, or verses, and soon
all that was left was *Tochter* and *Götterfunken*,
those soprano *A*s, over and over again.

Still the music never reached the end,
the coda and *A*s stretching to eternity,
as with Schumann, who was maddened
by that note, sirened by Angels into lunacy,

or those endless *As* in Shostakovich Five:
"You will rejoice, you will rejoice, you will rejoice,"
beating you with a Joy-stick till you're barely alive,
and you know you do not have a choice.

Poem reprinted in full due to error in Iota 88

Ginger

We knew some people who lived in a forest.
I was a small girl when we visited them –
friends of my parents.
There was melon. Everyone else
had powdered ginger on their melon
(including, as far as I remember, my elder brother).
But my mother said I was too young for ginger.
I didn't like the melon much anyway.
I liked the woman. She had eyes like a kitten's.
I liked her chintz, and her tales of wild ponies.
I liked her sweet delight in me –
it was the time when I was still cute.
It wasn't long before I got a lot spicier.

Naming of Parts
With thanks to Henry Reed.

Today we have naming of parts. Yesterday
we had daily hot flushes. And tomorrow morning
we shall have what to do with a migraine. But today,
today we have naming of parts. Wild Yam Root
is easily obtained from all of the health food shops,
and today we have naming of parts.

This is the right fallopian tube. And this
is the left fallopian tube, whose use you will lose,
now that you have arrived at the pause. And these are the ovaries,
which in your case you have not got. The Motherwort
grows in waste places and soothes uterine cramps,
which in our case we have not got.

This is the cervix, which is always smear-tested
once every three to five years. And please do not let me
see anyone missing their test. You can have it quite easy
if you spread your legs wide and relax. The Agnus Castus
acts on the pituitary and balances emotions, never letting anyone
miss their smear test.

And this you can see is the vagina. The purpose of this
is to allow easy access, as you can see. We can lubricate it
if it has dried due to lower oestrogen levels; we use this
gel called KY. And lubricating liberally with KY,
the man is fumbling and missing the clitoris,
while we notice loss of libido.

They call it loss of libido. It is perfectly easy
if you spread your legs wide and relax. Like the vulva,
and the cervix, the lubricating gel and the hormone levels,
which in our case we have not got; and the Black Cohosh
available in all of the health food shops and the man who is missing the point,
for today we have naming of parts.

David Holliday

Note on String Theory

Taut strings compel the marionette to dance
obedient to the hidden puppeteer,
as unseen powers cause us to advance
down ordained paths, as others may require.

Strings are the mainstay of the symphony,
from singing violins to thunderous bass.
All else supports with needful harmony,
with tonal colour and insistent pace.

And minute strings of energy vibrate
through multiple dimensions, giving rise
to basic particles, and so create
elements, planets, galaxies of stars.

David Holliday

Waiting Rooms

They come in various shapes and styles: ornate,
with gilded chairs and pictures on the walls
for such as bear attendance on the great;
or surgeries where anxious patients wait
the ominous moment when the doctor calls;
or hard seats in obscure and dusty rooms
for sinners who await the magistrate
- all places where the lesser congregate
to hear the greater weigh and speak their dooms.
And this house with its standard single cells,
its kindly carers, that they call a home....

Resonance

"There is no such thing as an empty space or an empty time....
In fact, try as we may to make a silence, we cannot."
--John Cage.

I

The vectors of this magnolia box, outlined
in curtained morn-light. Past the glass and plaster,
reveille of gulls echoes, from where the sole
sea is enclosed acres of furrows, green
carpeted; bell without tongue. All these dreams
can tell is that this will never be home.

II

The darkness curls out at the door's gaping.
A few steps in, something answers the hall-
light's flood.
                    Are you alright? Nerves freeze
until, like corridors' bare paths, this map
of air-duct hum
                         I know your absence – grain
and timbre, thick with needle-static; lack
of skin and spit; the radiator's shut-down
rattle. I'm quite the expert on it now.
And not so much a past confined to rough
upholstery, as present never become.

III

Of course, looking up from my coffee, bagel
and your booze-sticky table, you were joined
at the hand, fingers root-systems entwined,
and, further up, eyes coupled in dreaming
evasion. Each mouthful a little drier.

Your friend, who'd slurred at me from the lino,
preceded me out. *We should probably*
just leave them to it. Your goodbye, a leak
of dust, just barely registered. Outside
the stars still hid from me. I wished for *noir*,

gaslight, the consolation of drama;
the reel rolling to a close. Not as if
it was unknown, that we remain separate
species, no secret of uncoupled skin.
But still that proof's pore-traced violence lingers:

the friction of exploratory fingers,
the acid-burn of those upstanding hairs,
the contact sounding with scrape of flensed meat,
bone slashed to marrow. Knowledge of all skin
commits to ash. You remain, the unwitting.

And, taking still the night air, these words drift
and vanish like May pollen, as they should.
This place is now all your topography:
the chattering treetops, the black pavement –
and all as distant as the sky, shifting.

IV

And, crossing over, the fields opened up
before me, sound receding like warmth, pulse

with the houses, behind. Hedge-rustling. Fox
pausing, spark of immemory, twin orbs

as dark as earth; sly Reynard turning off
soundlessly. Grass half-felt, unheard, the dew

already crystallising, walking down.
And now, a stream's sweet gargle past the screen

of trees and gnarled mud path. Slowly, round
the border, fragments: chirp, trill, showers, Morse

code of woodnotes. The constellations bur-
ning into sound, tinkle of the broken

Godhead. The fractal silence, hearing, as
through stethoscopes, the sharp knocking of our

world, the intimate scraping of the spheres.

Mnemonics

I

The peeping eyes of my stone
collection wink at me across
the desk. The mottled, pitted basalt
plucked from the rust-spider of West Pier.
The aeon-thick sandwiches of
limestone, preserving fissures, harsh
radio-crackle, of Dancing
Ledge, Lizard Point, Hengistbury Head
barrow; bricks shattered, sculpted by
the sea's slow holocaust; potshards caught
in Brownsea clay. Measuring memory
in rock has advantages:
the living are always inundated;
the sea prospers over graves,
remembers better than touch.
Explains. Perhaps I knew, always
already, the hiss of life become
vanished – stars flickering to mineral;
the faces turned to shadows, stone
tongues in the story of rock.

II

Morse code
of sparrows on a TV fern
burst from a roof's white burial mound.
The Common's pleats of days-old snow
and its companion silence. 'Home'
I mutter, a word that stops
in this clear air: dead promise,
poet-chat, a known geography
of hearth-light, armchair, bedroom.
A knowing the world by proper names,
by words as easy as repose

in your presence. The rank and file
of the comforting dead audible
from mantelpiece photos, bough-song.
Wordless mornings, the old fear blares –
that your only holding is thought,
stony remnant. Your only gain
to pull it back to a grey breeze,
a window on slate roofs, a note-
book, this moment
                                        scrawling these words.

III

I try to keep in mind the buds
do not stay closed stone droplets always –
that I've seen summer's upswell, surge,
cells swollen, indiscreet with green.
And, once or twice, your life cracking
the caul, a gloss of copper nerves.
I shouldn't write that – I spent
too long putting you in well-lit rooms.
I keep busy enough, and with
better things than the heart. Love taught
me fuck all but for just how soon
calcification sets in,
the breathing stops and starts; how memory's
blank itch retains the only live
hypothesis. I have no right
to love you – and, handily,
I can't. But still the conjecture
persists: the slow dance of cells clotting;
breath's entrapped whisper; the threshold
strewn with May light, the world clamouring.

Julia Stothard

Forget-me-nots in the Wilderness

The neighbours have the sky in their garden;
self-seeded, uncultivated.
Their blossom clouding over the hedge
snows scent on our stony ground.

Our garden parades its regiments
I faithfully sowed indoors in March
tempted by the luscious wealth
of beans promised on glossy packets.

Sky-flowers walk the gaps
between our yellow patio slabs;
self-assured ambassadors
with their tiny breath of heaven,

whilst we agitate amongst the rows,
prising slugs from under stones.
In the street the Word is visiting
door-to-door. When they call at ours,

I tell them I don't believe -
but all about their feet
blue flowers wave to greet them;
self-seeded and persistent.

Displaced

Some part of her has come untied,
the loose ends trail through the night
as the hours widen, like a seam yielding
yawning its progress in degrees of fatigue.
Morning comes slowly; some manifestation
of her exits the house, hands
palming the front door closed
as if she were passing ex-lovers along
who never recall, never return.

In her white coat she crosses the road
into a ghost; a gust of cars blow past
giving her the illusion of movement.
She passes shop-fronts showing a slice
of what is inside, doorways facing the street
subdued. Cafés. She sees herself
through a window, alone
at a table for two, cross-threaded
into a life not entirely her own

where she meets herself in the wall's mirror,
staring through the base of a glass,
displaced and oddly distant. She has found
herself off-centre, swollen at the edges
from rubbing against convention, expectation –
a sore and sorry sight, stuck fast
in the bottle-neck between her past
and her future. In the last effort of daylight
she walks back to where she began,

catches the blade on the clock-tower face
chopping up seconds to throw away:
The deaths already named around the base
remind her, returning home each day.
As the door snips shut behind her,
it cuts off to her private space, backlit, exposed:

The silhouette of what she ought to be
heading towards her dreams.
She keeps seeing what could be beautiful,
if only she could reach it.

Spinning Plates

My mother was mad as mercury,
mad as a silken Disraeli stovepipe
hat hiding a gypsum-white rabbit.

She once told me, the malt talking,
that I wasn't her first born boy,
there had been seminal drafts.

She said that being pregnant
was like spinning a bone-china plate
on the thinnest stick inside you.

Breakages were bound to occur.
It was a question of which piece
could drop intact and roll around

on a hardwood floor, its rim ringing
with cries. My sister is an artisan
firing, a wild coloured plate

still atwirl. I am a white canteen
saucer, ready to be tanned with tea-
slops. A cupped palm for spillages.

The Estate

The milk is souring in the fridge
along with your opinion of me.
Your heart is the derelict miners
welfare club down the road.

Neither pint nor tea will slake
this thirst to stay on the 29 bus
one stop beyond my destination
where I work a custodial job.

I want the old Leyland beast to chug
down into another dog-shit common
with a septic beck oozing through.
I'll alight and scout out the local

then stagger across to the estate,
a terrace where there's a bed going,
a place of Christmas decorations
that are autumnally precocious.

The Sin-Eaters at John's Send-Off

The Stormont Main was a poor-man's Hades
that pallid afternoon, all matchstick sulphur
with the *de profundis* of a clear Toon defeat
and slow oblivion in pints of Double Maxim.

John's bereaved found good dour company
in those barstool footballers. Soon the bait
was laid and plonkie, mourner and grim-eater
had salmon sarnies bought by the dearly departed.

There was enough grief in that fermented room
to colour a penny-black and among stale crusts
I was reminded of those medieval tramps, called
for from darkest dells to eat sins from a still chest.

The Men in the Background

We are always there, but you don't see us
because your gaze is disrobing her,
uniting them – we've seen you looking.
We might be smoking, we might be reading
or earning our keep by cutting the grass,
our poses counterbalance
the action in the foreground.
We are the scene-shifters, the dirt-diggers,
the shit-shovellers, shape-shifting
through all paintings, touching
and tweaking each scene until
it's right. We are the great unwashed
at the back, the sanitised poor,
ignorant, all-knowing and dumb,
anticipating the artist's needs.
We are plain, washed out and bland,
our faces daubed on, undefined,
an afterthought. You won't know
us when we pass in the street –
but we'll know you, we always do.

You Hated Those Plums

They frightened you, the plums
I bought; the blood-raw hue,
foreign skin, the wet
of the edges where I cut one open
and displayed it like two chambers
of a heart. Forgive me –
I didn't mean to kickstart
your tension headache.
I was at home with them –
childhood memories
of skinning knees as I climbed
the tree to pick them.
I should not have played that trick
and peeled one, cold from the fridge,
while, eyes closed, you held out your palm
so you thought you were nursing
an eyeball. Wide-eyed, you caught
the stains on my hands
as if I were Lady Macbeth.
I'm so very sorry. I can't explain –
I'll go now and buy apples,
a punnet of peaches, or chance you
with a mango, you new soul,
you greenhorn, you remarkable fruit virgin.

Modus Operandi

This is where the choice is made,
in the dark, in the noise;
he has singled her out, here
where the throb of the bass
forces him closer, beer breath
in her ear, the sharp tang
of perspiration surrounds him.
-What's your name, by the way?
He has chosen her, from all the girls
in little clothes, enjoying cheap drinks
for 'the ladies'.
She hasn't checked for hair
on his palms, his indoor complexion
intrigues more than frightens.
She hasn't checked for a weapon,
doesn't know what method
he will use, can't read his mind,
just his body, which makes clear
his intention.
So she answers in a pale voice,
not seeing his sharp teeth,
the way his hands are clasped,
their knuckles white, the sweat
on his top lip.
The he asks simply:
-Are you on your own? Can I buy you a drink?
and that's how it starts,
how things are made and shaped,
how we craft our lives by casual conversations,
not knowing or thinking what comes next,
not grasping the danger
of how words can be angled.

Black Sun

We are down in the dumps.
With no redemptive gleam to the hill of bin bags,
the kind tears can blur and divide into coins.

So what do we expect of each other –
a *purpureus pannus*, the meaning of moaning?
Perhaps a sight of the sea between poured concrete

is something the touch of my hand
on your shoulder may yet articulate.
But it's getting dark and the rats are about

by which I mean the screenwriters
insisting this scene we're having
should begin late and end early

with much tearful muttering and turning away
to the window and yelling at each other
and immediately apologising.

Help me up, would you love,
from the space-age debris
of tomorrow's attempt to save face?

Vidyan Ravinthiran

Swing State

When the storm burst over the terrace and the sea
did a Fosbury flop into the hotel swimming pool
and the palm trees out on the tiles that night bent forward
like native women drying their hair on the ground
or Draupadi washing her hair in Dusshasana's blood,
it was the roar of the beast we heard in our room
as huge flakes of white paint like the dandruff of gods
tore from the walls and ceiling to land in our laps.
Though I have also heard, closer to home,
the purr of some great power in those birches
the wind fills gently as we say fine things;
unmissable, gripping, of a blistering intensity
dawn marks the face of the red-brick opposite
like a bloody pawprint, or the hi-def glow of fur
as it breaks, in slow-motion, gazelles in half.
And when we made one composite sweating animal
on the bed or arguing policy over brandy and cigars
it was possible to believe, for those few minutes,
we were in the very engine-room of the creature,
that its cries were our cries and its violence
the consummation of our conflicting desires.
With so much glass and steel probing the sky
it's hard to see which way the wind is blowing;
perhaps a cadre of reptilians in a sky-box
have evolved, of hoods and codes, a machine
whose amiable growl the small bones of the ear
process in the dead of night? The purple passage
threads institutions on its way to the graveyard;
a fine mist lifted off its windows by the sunlight,
a gaggle of exiled smokers smoke in front of the tower
which therefore looks like it, itself, is smoking.
I saw something like that once in Kentucky, a waterfall
with a great dark cave beneath with a giant in it
puffing away at his pipe whose fumes were churned up spray
encoding a spectrum in daylight, the rare moonbow
certain nights of the year. You could get paranoid
about him putting it all on for our benefit; or,
as Obama and Cameron tread cautiously on BP
listen to a dry leaf skittering over the flags
like the nail your whimpering boxer wouldn't have cut.

Recession

Down an iron spiral staircase like a trilobite,
remembering aggrieved suits at the bar,
past shanties painted gaily, fooling no one
we arrive in the dishevelment of our aspirations

at the square of this ghost town where the dust
comes at you breast-high, like the swimming pool
one's back yard used to boast, a blue stone
of the finest water. The built landscape

in our heads could not, after all, be numbered
reliably as our hairs; lucky for some,
the automatic elegance of phrasing
a salary in the low six figures will transmit

to its blasé dependents, blessed with a sense
that any room they enter is all ears
tuned in to their nice discriminations...
A boho hobo tweets his blues up the stairwell.

Dot Dot Dot

After dinner we see a fingerprint
lifted, germ-luminous, off the guilty surface;
another leaps from the victim's thigh
like the bright bands of a bee
and fairly zooms at the eye, as if saying
the wackos were right, steel wouldn't melt

at that temperature, and yes, everyone hates you...
That night, I dream an avenue of limes
at dusk, odorous, wondering
what exactly it is I'm advertising
before I realise I can't know exactly
how each leaf looks on each tree –

I might as well number the telogen hairs
responsible for our flooding shower,
the bezoars of our couplehood
one may only lift from the plughole
with a beckoning finger, as if trying
for the fabled G-spot...

Apollinaire's Pornography

Masturbation is an admirable thing, for it allows men and women to become accustomed to their imminent and prolonged separation.
– Guillaume Apollinaire, Les Onze Mille Verges

What night remains he spends on tenterhooks.
Moraine of underthings. The house itself
can't sleep for satin, jealous static, sex-smells.

Skinflint voyeur, he types up lies he thinks
might turn her on: two men and her, him with another girl.
Their lives will test the limits of invention.

Love is penurious, poetry either the old sob-story,
or too much like hard work. Pornography
is a modern creature, like a Zeppelin,

or an ocean liner fitted as a hospital
where nurses flit like ghosts between the bulkheads,
unbandaging and probing open wounds.

Hokusai

Pushing eighty, this old man daft for art
hikes across the island to paint waves.

Finally, he thinks, mastery of his craft
is within reach – at worst, another thirty years

of looking and thinking. His eyesight's good,
his head as clear as it ever was. Still,

these waves might be his last, so he decides
to paint them male and female, tickled

to have them locked in separate panels,
all turmoil and frustration and raw difference.

You couldn't fish for tuna in those seas,
he thinks. He thinks: too many wives, he's

grown too cynical. And yet he can't resist
the colours brought from Europe, as he once

could not resist a pretty girl – that's gone,
he notes, that old libidinous get-up-and-go,

he's finally shed at least that much desire –
and any bitter taste is sluiced away by tides

of mauve and jewelled reds from England's
factories, of oceanic blues and greens...

He tells himself: *when I'm a hundred I shall be*
a marvellous artist, and after I am dead

a Will o' the wisp taking it easy in the dark,
always in the next field, and then the next,

while more and more often, foreigners dock
their tall ships in the harbours of Japan.

Radio Ulster News

I was leaving no stone unturned in my granny's bedroom,
in search of the savings the old cow had salted away

against the expense of her pauper's funeral,
when the radio said that the body dragged from the river

and decayed almost beyond identification
was that of my half-brother, missing these three years

ever since he'd been given his marching orders
by my father-in-law, his wife, and the rest of the boys.

The Architecture of Fire Stations

You know those hollow towers and folding
fortress doors, wide turning circles:
formal, yet common; welcoming but stern.

You know the coarse, pragmatic optimism
of the will with which the concrete's poured.
The ribbon-cutting. Will we never learn?

And know our love affairs have been like this,
built from hard-earned experience,
and each time better. Still our houses burn.

Interviews

Mario Petrucci

Poet, educator, songwriter and eco-physicist Mario Petrucci is renowned for combining innovation and linguistic excitement with a profoundly human aspect. He has been a Bridport winner, a prizewinner in the National Poetry Competition, four times winner of the London Writers Competition, and a Royal Literary Fund Fellow. The only poet to have held residencies at the Imperial War Museum and with BBC Radio 3, Petrucci contributes widely to poetry in the public domain (the Royal Society, the Natural History and Dickens Museums, Southwell Workhouse). *Flowers of Sulphur* (Enitharmon, 2007) gained an Arts Council England Writers' Award and a New London Writers Award, while his Arvon-winning *Heavy Water: a poem for Chernobyl* (Enitharmon, 2004) led to an internationally acclaimed film (Seventh Art Productions). "One of the best poets of our times" (*Literati*), Petrucci generates "Poetry on a geological scale... a new track for poets of witness" (*Verse*). *i tulips* (Enitharmon, 2010) promises "a truly ambitious landmark body of work" (*PBS Bulletin*). www.mariopetrucci.com

---

I'm reading your newest book, *i tulips*: this is something very different for you, in form and in scope. Can you say where it started?

Not so new, perhaps, Angela. Recently, I've been finding prototypic *i tulips* poems - or segments of poems - in some of my earliest writing. I suppose your question might be easier to address if I could be sure your readers knew more or less where I was (in terms of style and approach) pre-*tulips*. And you're touching here on a fascinating world few readers ever see: what motivates and moulds the progression of the writer behind the tangible evidence of his or her books. I love finding out about that myself, for other writers (it's one of the great rewards of mentoring). So, with all that in mind, I might go on a bit!

Perhaps my first full collection *Shrapnel and Sheets* (Headland, 1996) is as good a place as any to start. You might describe it as a themed collection of strongly wrought, intense poems concerned with childhood and family, bereavement, love, Italy / The War, and science / medical science, along with a mix of political, historical and social phenomena that happened to take me. As with many contemporary collections of poetry, I was moving through my work, more or less, poem by isolated poem, adapting or inventing forms and approaches for each matter in hand. Many of those poems had been thoroughly workshopped, often several times, and put through a stringent peer-assisted redrafting process (usually varying in intensity according to each poem's perceived inadequacies and potential rewards) to get just the right, pared-down and essential effect appropriate to the individual poem in terms of eliminating infelicities and maximising impact.

But there was a problem. Several colleagues pointed out my ongoing tendency to overwrite, to become engrossed in the tumbling of imagery through different registers. Those many workshops (plus several incredibly patient colleagues) acted as compensation, helping me to spot flaws in my design or exposition, to see where my imagistic horses were pulling in too many directions. It was pretty hard work getting it all just so; but I was determined to achieve the optimal poem, however painful the process or partial the results. There were quite a few competition wins, though, and I began to harbour an image of myself as a writer who, in the long term, would eventually understand his craft and weaknesses to such a degree that he'd produce at a consistently high level and – who knows? – might even become the vehicle for a few great poems.

Privately, though, I was vaguely dissatisfied: there was a kind of exasperation with my own instincts, as though I sensed that the ideal (hugely trained and *made*) writer I hoped to be was one who'd never quite sit well with my marrow. I recall friend and collaborator Martyn Crucefix suggesting (in what was probably a vital moment) that maybe it wasn't just the paring and checking that I needed to pursue; perhaps I should seek a way of working *with* my nature, finding modes of composition that could accommodate the imagistic, verbal rush, that would allow my propensity for a densely imagistic and discursive metaphysics to flower. Not pruning, then, but fertilising. That small spigot of insightful and unexpected advice probably played a part in piquing my desire to access the entire linguistic barrel. It's what every writer has to do: constantly grow away from their own rootstock without altogether losing sight of what the roots taught them. But how was I to do that, emphatically, without becoming wilfully obscure or impenetrably wrapped up in my own contexts, concerns and biography?

Did asking yourself that question result in a turning point for you?

It was a question, perhaps, that I'd always put to myself, in one form or another; but it wasn't until a particular period in 2005, when I'd been reading American modernist poets of the last mid-century, that a radically fresh trajectory finally seemed to resolve in me in terms of confidence and intention. There'd been early flares that something was coming, like electrical 'spikes' in a circuit that's firing up. One of these, a short sequence entitled *Nights*, has only now been published (October 2010) by Flarestack. Around the time I wrote *Nights*, I was coming powerfully under the influence of 'Black Mountain' – a term, like many literary labels, so fuzzy and questionable as to be of modest value, perhaps, only when first approaching the subject. One thinks, though, of such poets as Charles Olson, Robert Creeley (how wonderfully idiosyncratically he reads aloud!), maybe Robert Duncan and (by very loose association) Denise Levertov, and, over here, Roy Fisher – poets for whom, put (over-)simply, one perception leads immediately and directly into the next. I found my own 'British' (or is it European?) interpretation of their collective and highly differentiated drive, whilst leaning heavily on Olson's famous linking of thought (via the ear) to the syllable and emotion (via the breath) to the line. I sought an improvised form that carried an organic unity with content and, crucially, a firm emphasis on the opportunities afforded by the line break. I was inspired, too, by the 'Objectivists' – another fraught term, centred on the likes of George Oppen and Louis Zukofsky, but also associated with William Carlos Williams and (arguably) Basil Bunting. Here I gained a sensitivity to poems/ words as actualised objects, became more alert to the significance of small and ordinary words (including the definite/ indefinite article), and squared up to the notion of The World As It Is. There was/ is a usefully strong sense in me, also, of the New York School (Ashbery, O'Hara, etc.), plus a dash of cummings, and an attraction to the oddly striding, formally tight, extensive confessionalism and wrenched syntax of Berryman's *Dream Songs*.

It's tempting, isn't it, for us to stay in our comfort zones? Especially when it has led to some success. Was it difficult for you to push in a new direction, and what did that new direction involve?

Difficult? Yes and No. We often associate change with greater, more intense application; but such shifts as these may have more to do with retuning your sensitivities and sensibilities (not always a complete rewiring job) or with 'getting out of the way'. It might be about letting the 'work' happen *to* or *in* you. I admit, you might need to focus fairly intently, at times, on your habits of perception and approach, to either quell, overcome, or (less confrontationally) transform them. In this, a fresh reading list (or a freshly *perceived* existing list) can be crucial. Much of my own reorientation in reading and poetic deliberation was spurred and assisted by my long-term friend and co-editor at Perdika Press, Peter Brennan. Peter knows all one needs to know about the modernist heave away from convention, and much of his aesthetic chimed in with and supported my own. His encouragement and guidance (backed by his ongoing attentiveness to my progression as a writer) when I was veering away from what I knew (and knew would be acceptable to the mainstream) was timely, to say the least.

So, I found myself gazing across the Pond. But behind all that (mostly) American energy was my own enduring connection with an accessible 'British' lyricism, though somewhat tempered and pressurised by a psychological and metaphysical richness I admired in, say, Rilke. So, the subjects of these new poems are more pliable, more complex perhaps, than most of *Shrapnel and Sheets.* They don't slip (as much) into that contemporary habit of leading the reader by the hand carefully through the poem, signposting and framing the poem's moments of significance. *i tulips* aims less to talk a*bout* things than to speak *through* experience, association and sound: language not so much as mere medium for content, but as active participant in thought and feeling; or language as a vehicle, perhaps, but geared towards something 'else' (what all great writing, as far as I'm concerned, must aspire to) outside or beyond experience, behind language. That's a pretty intimidating prospect at first; but eventually it comes to embrace you. It's not a case of dumping your unprocessed notebooks on the public... rather, it's a preparedness to receive poems by a different route. So, poetry can arrive like dictation from another linguistic dimension. I've found this new approach astonishingly liberating, in ways that I hope will be communicated to the open-minded (and open-eared) reader – not as 'difficulty' or randomness, but as a layeredness authentic to experience, a shifting, challenged coalition (if not unity) of meaning and sound. But always, at the heart of this: humanity, love, felt reality.

One of my first compositions consciously in this new style was partly in imitation of Creeley. It really got things moving for me, as if I'd finally decoded a vitally unlocking portion of my own Rosetta Stone. Since then, there've been over 800 poems in *i tulips* mode, often streamed into subtly recognisable strands of style, subject, manner and tone. But, as I said earlier, there were clear precursors. Most of *Shrapnel and Sheets* sounds like this (taken at random):

> "And then the man laid out –
> chins like gills, skin
> yellow as last year's papers..."
>
> *'Before Your Time'*

... but you'll find the odd bit of proto-*i tulips* there too:

> "*girls with waists like water   the rim*
> *of a well   smell of night-time harbour...*"
>
> *'Duende'*

I suppose the acorn really does contain the oak.

So, with over 800 poems behind the *i tulips* project, do you consider them to be separate poems? A single poem? A sequence?

I've only recently begun studying Jack Spicer (of the 'San Francisco Renaissance') and his theories of poetry: most of *i tulips* runs quite close to his idea of the 'serial poem'. This has the book (or, in my case, the poetic project) as its unit, with its sub-unit the poem arrived at by taking a kind of dictation, without looking back or changing what you've done, gone into "not knowing what the hell you're doing" – indeed, "you have to be tricked into it" [Spicer].

In that state of surrender, belief and faith become their own engine. It's almost a kind of perpetual motion, only here the 'impossible' can happen: not the miracles of literature's Old Testament, but those of the New. In this way of thinking and writing, the editing process is often minimal, since the entire poem – line by line, syllable by syllable – evolves through and with the form. It's true that *i tulips* offers an overarching sense of invented form that helps to bind the poems together; but the sequence, for all its recurrences, also gives rise to utter individualism in the poems, not only in terms of the moment in which they came to be, but also by virtue of how they place themselves within that binding energy of the sequence.

What *is* that linking sense of form in *i tulips*?

It mostly revolves around what I call 'bevelled tercets'. Just a glance at the poems makes clear, I think, what I mean by that. I'm still not sure quite how I arrived at it. Perhaps there was some Platonic ideal hovering somewhere that decided to ground itself through me.

What issues arose in your attempts to ground that ideal?

I realised at some point, and in my own way, that when you strike towards – or into – a new creative mode, you have to find ways and techniques to stay connected to yourself while articulating and exploring the potencies and transcendent potentials of language. You have to remain as steady as you are lissom. That's not to say you really know, cognitively, what you're doing, or can work it all out... the enterprise is more akin to Keats' Negative Capability, or meditation. I suppose what I've learned is that we need each other, but must always be testing and transcending that need. It's like parenting yourself, knowing when to move on from dependency into your own metamorphosis. You still listen, and attend to criticism; but it no longer determines who you are. So, I don't attend workshops anymore, and the workshops I run are (I hope) about as far as you can get from polishing the next competition entry via rigid workshoppy ideas. I've become far more interested in the deeper, riskier aspects of the writing process. How can we relate and engage in that much bigger (often less well-lit) space? Ultimately, you have to find your own way to yourself. That's what *i tulips* seems to have become for me: a way of being sympathetic not just with a subject, but also with myself. And now that I really think about it, the shorter answer to your question concerning 'where it started' might be to say that it starts again, in the present tense, with every moment.

You said earlier that 'the editing process is often minimal'. I'm guessing that's different from your usual (or 'old') way of working? Can you identify other differences in your writing process between *i tulips* and the earlier work?

I'd stress, I think, the revelatory aspect in *i tulips*, which encompasses more than the deployment of felicitous images and phrases in a poem? Another thought: rather than merely reacting to the desire to write well *about* a particular something, it's the pressure of the 'Gestalt' – that 'something in general' – that primes and pumps your pen. There's kinship, here, with automatic writing and stream of consciousness – but more ordered, maybe, than those often are. One ordering principle is that I'll often have a 'keying' idea hovering behind the composition – usually a scientific fact or metaphysical insight. So, one writes/ injects *into* the chosen form, with the form moulding the input whilst being itself remoulded (if necessary) by the input pressure. It's certainly a profound 'listening as you go', opposed (if 'opposition' is the right notion here) to the common methodology of iterating your way towards a final draft through various stages of stanzaic quilt-making and the canny orchestration of images whose aim is to make the driving idea clear and calculable. Charles Bernstein says of Louis Zukofsky's poems that they "are not representations of ideas but enactments of thoughts in motion, articulated as sound"; or, more warmly, that "when we hold them in our hands we see our hands". There is a "refusal to separate... complexity from clarity". Even Larkin commented that poets shouldn't "deal in instant emotion, instant opinion, instant sound and fury" – though I doubt, somehow, he'd approve of the ways in which I interpret his injunction.

That said, each particular process, each *tulip*, is its own story, its own spokesperson. Actually, I shouldn't be acting here as interpreter – it risks misunderstanding, for a start. Moreover, I'm not really in analytical mode while these poems are being written; there just isn't the same 'serialised' inspection process between drafts to plot out on any 'process axis'. Like experience itself, the writing of the poem *happens* (not entirely unlike Allan Kaprow's artworks or the efforts of the Wiener Gruppe), though you may (or may not) reflect on it later to engage in some tinkering. Indeed, there's a feeling that the untouched poem, or line, however imperfect, may sometimes be the better record of the lived experience it relates? What's certain is that the *i tulips* poems, overall, have been less interfered with, less 'prepared' for the public, than many earlier published pieces were. I see now that previous poems (where redrafting and peer comment were usually core process factors in terms of how they evolved) reflect a different mosaic of experiences to that of a poem 'happening' at the end of a pen or through a keyboard: the editorial input in the former case is, I think, a much larger part of what the reader experiences, though it's often fairly invisible (i.e. not consciously witnessed at the poem's surface).

For *i tulips*, then, interested readers might discover more of the 'emergent process' – and more availably, perhaps – in the poems themselves? I certainly hope they'll be implicated in that process, allowing themselves to be caught up in part-inventing the meaning. Of course, some readers are reluctant to do any such work, or just aren't prepared to delay gratification; others might dismiss *i tulips* by association with what they perceive, rightly or wrongly, as wilful obscurity or pointlessly impenetrable 'difficulty' on the part of certain authors they've previously read. There's also a strange assumption (I make it too, to an extent) that an invitation to greater reader involvement in a text must be accompanied by less pleasure in the poem as immediately read. But what I'm after is an enrichment of *all* the strata of a poem, not just a frisson in the depths at the expense of the presented surface. As illustration, here are a few lines from *Shrapnel and Sheets* (1996):

> *Opened my eyes to my husband's bed, the room*
> *just one chair, a slow clock. Shutters admitted*
> *slats of first light - water on stucco. The crude*
> *pine headboard wafted its incense. His dark head.*
>
> from '*Sheets*'

... and, for contrast, from *i tulips* (2010):

> *oh* ill walk that
> negative self down the
>
> road invisible against
> asphalt – this old body t-
> urned antimatter ganger &
>
> all honest tumour except
> for will in its two b-
> right halves &
>
> under its rib that un-
> stoppable fib-
> rillant
>
> muscle
>
> from '*one pink heart*'

Does the example help at all? See, for instance, how the rhythm and meaning in the second piece jostle with line breaks and hyphenations, complicating but (also, I hope) enriching the meaning. What I seek are those processes in writing that open up both author and reader to profounder possibilities in language than one usually finds in the well-turned poem that delivers a series of messages and effects with relative reproducibility and aesthetic/pictorial accuracy. I'm not knocking that (latter) approach *per se*, but suggesting there are other ways to generate a reading experience of immense value, ways that can begin to access certain 'codes' and modes in language that a more conventional poem (whatever that means) may struggle to reach. A beautiful or emphatic poem that presents a tidy unity according to pre-set ideas or etiquettes is fine, if that's what you want from art; I want to be beautiful and emphatic too; but these newer poems also explore a variety of effects and stimulations that will be more difficult for most reading groups or workshops to define or confine. They pursue a plural, layered conception of those encounters we experience in ourselves through language in the midst of lived moments, language that attempts to engage with the imagination *in motion*. I still want the text, though, to be utterly readable, potent in the ear, relevant to heart as well as mind.

So, to return to your question more explicitly, I suppose the essential difference between *i tulips* and what came before involves (to varying degrees) an attempt to *enact* experience rather than to merely comment upon it, combined with the sense that words themselves are at the centre of our experience of words.

Thank you for your time, Mario. There are threads in what you've said that I'd love to follow up, but we're out of space – so, I'll just ask what you see as your next step in these explorations?

In a way, time belongs to us all – so, no need for thanks. And I appreciate your questions! As for *i tulips*, I'm aiming to stop at 1001 poems. I figure, by then, it'll be visible from space. But look at what happened to Pound with his Cantos – I think I read somewhere that he thought they'd end at 100...? Meanwhile, the real exploration is life: family, friends, making one's way with integrity. Not being a tourist in your own consciousness. Keeping the channels of language open will be part of that, I'm pretty sure, wherever I'm taken. In terms of words, I'll keep listening for the goat bells that tinkle through the night, and just do my best to try to glimpse where the craft and the graft require me to be.

this light shows

through you as dusk
where you turn
addressing

addressed
by our window
as though you wore

gauze of being here
more lightly when
i yearn through

you for light
beyond you yet
i learn the firmest

sight can hold onto
tonight is that
shaping &

shaped-by
almost-here
fern-coloured

dress

from *i tulips* (Enitharmon, 2010)

everyone begins as fish &

ends so – spiralling after
egg (that other half of our
chains) & setting gills

in gristled knot that buds
legs as tadpoles do & blow-
hole ears halfway down

the back & low-set eye
alien as featherless chick –
ah we have peered into

that shared ovum whose
blasto-flesh runs its gauntlet
of fowl & fish so fused at

the tail nothing can be told
apart – is this why when i am
late i find in upstairs dark

you – on placenta duvet &
hunched round self as wom-
bed ones are? – as though

i had just returned from
all eternity to catch you
naked out sleepwalking

space without even
navel-twisted purpled
rope to hold you

from *i tulips* (Enitharmon, 2010)

for a newborn son

what pours

from that so-fast
treading there
just under

where rib
might be – your
one tight curd in muscle

throwing itself back &
through & always
back angry

with life
it fills with or
empties hung in

you as a red wasp
in almost too
small

a web?

from *crib* (forthcoming, Enitharmon)

Sheets
(Italy, 1944)

that stripping down – selves mothers heirs
daughters / sons made a bed their blood
coverlets pretended white laid
down to sleep pillows the unborn
who reach through those pink shapes vaguely
curious their feathered arms out
-stretched as just beyond night's glass they
can barely see fall snows piling
white from pitch as though all mothers
do is bonfire sheets   the down they
put here as tiny hands or feet

from *the waltz in my blood* (forthcoming, Waterloo Press)

Carol Rumens

is the author of fifteen collections of poems, among them *Poems, 1968-2004* (Bloodaxe Books), *Blind Spots* (Seren, 2008) and *De Chirico's Threads* (Seren, 2010). She has published occasional fiction, including a novel, *Plato Park* (Chatto, 1987) and she has recently completed a new novel. She has had several plays produced. Her translations of Russian poets (Pushkin, Yevgeny Rein, Kudriavitsky, Ratushinskata, etc.) appear in various anthologies, and her own poems are translated into Polish, Romanian, Russian and French.

She has received the Cholmondeley Award and the Prudence Farmer Prize, and was joint recipient of an Alice Hunt Bartlett Award. Her most recent prose publication is *Self into Song* (2007) based on three poetry lectures delivered in the Bloodaxe-Newcastle University Lecture Series. She has edited several anthologies, the most recent being an anthology of work by poets associated with Hull, *Old City: New Rumours* (Five Leaves, 2010), co-edited with Ian Gregson.

She was Director of the Philip Larkin Centre for Poetry and Creative Writing at the University of Hull between 2005-6, and is now a part-time Professor of Creative Writing at the University of Bangor and Visiting Professor of Creative Writing at the University of Hull. She is currently a judge of the Eric Gregory Awards, and a Fellow of the Royal Society of Literature.

It is apparent from your books that you work comfortably in a wide variety of forms. At what stage, in the making of a poem, do you know what its form will be?

It depends on the poem. Some poems have begun with a preoccupation with a set form, almost an obsession. This might go on for a long time, and give rise to scribblings that don't add up to poems at all, only rackety technical constructions with the wires sticking out and the supports collapsing. But, finally, the set of patterns a particular form embodies will sink to a subconscious level, and that's when it's ready to be grown organically into a poem. And then you feel as if these set-form-poems are pre-set! They bring the form along with them: it's as if they made the choice, not the poet.

But of course form is bigger than the set forms (of which there are relatively few, and most of which are imports into English). Many contemporary poems are one-offs. I both love and hate this freedom. At the moment I find I'm tending to write in the unguarded way, following where the poem leads - at least, up to a point. There is always control, some of it conscious, most of it subliminal. Lineation is micro-form: I worry all the time about the shape of the line, its drama, its flow and pauses, the syntax, the tone. Even when lines come very naturally (perhaps especially then) I question them once they're written down. I think that form evolves from listening to the sounds and seeing the pictures and feeling the textures you make, and judging their effectiveness together. A poem is a multi-media object, even if it's only lying flat on the page. That heady mixture is its form. But you can't get there before you've written, and re-written, the poem. Whether free or formal, poems need growing time. A set form is never a short-cut, although sometimes it kids you that it will be.
It never is.

You say "the set of patterns a particular form embodies will sink to a subconscious level": does anything similar happen with free verse? Can you identify any difference in your process when working with forms or free verse?

I think I have a deep imprint of iambic pentameter. It's regrettable. When I write free verse the subconscious impulse is to hear the line against this metrical grid, even if subdivided. So I try to push myself against that tendency.

Another obstacle is the temptation to what I call lineation-by-clause. I think it produces boring poetry, even when the author is Ted Hughes! So I think about ways of avoiding this, and then of course face the problem of un-natural jolts. Odd line-breaks need to have a reason. Writing free verse is an anxious process for me, but there are rewards. You can change pace more frequently, dramatise images more emphatically. The risk is that these devices will seem cheap and obvious.

I'm not sure if free verse really does belong to the genre, poetry. It's accepted by all but the stuffiest convention that it does. I'm not stuffy, I hope, but I like precision, and I think one of the reasons modern poetry is so little, and so poorly, discussed, is that it's run on ahead of any descriptive or critical language. That doesn't mean you can't have very effective writing in the prose-poem or «prosical» style. Going back to the translations of the Psalms and rushing on with the Imagists, there's a wonderful tradition of free writing in English. H.D., Pound's Li Po translations, Sylvia Plath in Ariel, Lowell's Life Studies - these would be some touch-stones. If I could get something as alive as those rhythms in my head and my verse I'd be thrilled. In writing formally, there are as many processes as forms, probably. I've never had a sestina-shaped thought, though I've written sestinas! It's all very improvisatory and open, despite the repetons, and also because of them. But I have had a sonnet-shaped thought, a villanelle-shaped thought. The poem as it grows will alter that thought, of course, but it won't run off with it as a longer, complicated form might.

I like symmetry, and I like patterns-within-patterns. To write in form in the larger sense (not a set-form, but one that to some degree exploits expectations and regularities), and to devise those patterns as the poem develops, is the way of writing that gives me most pleasure. And in the end that's the best reason for writing. Pleasure - and challenge. You don't want it to be either a complete torment or a package holiday!

You mention 'growing time' for poems, how much is revision and rewriting part of that growing time? Do you see revision as a separate process to the initial drafting, or part of the same process?

It's part of the same process. I revise poems before they're typed. Then again, after. And so on, for as long as it takes. It's all the same process. If something goes seriously wrong, then I go back to the first scribbly draft, if I haven't mislaid it. I feel that all the seeds are there- the shape may be vague, the language may be too loose, but there's always the hint of the solution, the completion. The finished form is embedded –or casts its shadow - somewhere.

The presence of the finished form's seeds or shadow is intriguing; is it there from the beginning, from the first hint of a poem's genesis? How does a poem usually begin, for you?

I don't want to be mystical about it, and maybe it's only with hindsight I find the seeds of the form were always there in a poem. So much of the process of writing is playing around, trying things out, letting one thing suggest another, and then getting rid of what doesn't work. A poem often begins with very little - a few lines that contain some kind of strong feeling: there would be a rhythm, of course and at least one image which had narrative potential or seemed worth developing. What I've just been reading, what I've just been thinking about, probably gets in at some stage, and each time I re-draft I'll see another connection I could make. If it finally works out, the form will seem to have been inevitable, but perhaps that's an illusion!

I'd like to ask about the verse play in your new book, *De Chirico's Threads (also the title of the book)*: How did this come about – why a verse play, rather than any other form? How long have you been working on it?

I like De Chirico's early work, and had reconnected with it via Margaret Crosland's biography, but felt that it was too easy to respond only in poems. And then I saw a competition for a verse-play, so that was my excuse. I thought I'd try one about De Chirico, showing how he struggles to redefine himself as an artist over a long career.

I've written in the genre before, but never published anything.

The play wasn't a winner, and its presence in the book has probably ensured that no-one reads or reviews it. .Most people who have commented don't seem to have a clue what it's about. But it's not written in a surreal or arcane style, is it?

This is what Anne Stevenson wrote:

"I have to confess I am having difficulty understanding your De Chirico's Threads. Surrealism has never pretended to be anything but a dream, though a symbolic one, I suppose. Can you give me some idea of how you thought of it?"

I can't say I had a problem with the verse-play, finding it neither surreal nor arcane in style. I can imagine it doing well on the radio because the soundscape of it works so well - not surprisingly, given your obvious attention to sound in your other poems. Is sound an intrinsic part of the making of a poem for you – is it a consideration from the beginning, or a stage in revision?

Thanks for the encouraging comment on play. I think sound matters more than anything. I hear poems as I write them, and often say them aloud. But I don't have a system - the judgement is completely subjective and intuitive as to whether it sounds good or not. I guess sound is a kind of additional form.

So finally, what's next? Are you working on something or do you find the need for a fallow period after a book release?

Next on my list is, first, to do more translation. I'd like to add to the single canto from Dante's Purgatorio which I completed over the summer! Also, I want to get together some of my blogs, reviews and critical bits and pieces for a book about poetry. I completed a novel a while back, which I need to shorten before trying to find a publisher.

Poems happen as and when...I've never had a strategy, rarely ever planned a book as a whole connected project. I should, I know, but my brain (or whatever is involved) doesn't work at poems like that.

Ancient Lovers
(Figurine, calcite, c.8000 B.C., Ain Sahkri)

1.
They've formed a heart, their heads
its atria, their torsos
fused and veined - a little, rooted heart,
small as a lamb's, flickering
into motion at the sounds
of our own moved hearts nearby.
Their mouths and noses puzzle
together: kiss or breathe?

2.
Was it simply a pouch of charms
for the skinny teenaged goddess
of the wandering barley -
or a 'Valentine' for a sullen rain-god - simply?

3.
In the River that Made the World, an eye
picked out the cobble.
It pressed a thirsty taste against the tongue.
In the palm, it made a soft fist.
The tired eye went deeper
into the grey-white shadow, looking for
the future ghosted there.

When he and she were already a memory
he or she held fast this remembering stone.

4.
Stone:
it shivers a little, readies itself
for ruin or transformation,
warms, dampens, as she
or he revolves it, scrapes it, pauses, probes
the faintly moist and glittery
grain of the calcite, feeling

no melt-water rush through cervix
or glans, not that - or only
the faintest
tiny scald - but trusting unseen culverts
into the hand, into the tipped
flint, machining now the heart of the stone.

5.
Not all the breathing-to-breathing
not all the clench of thigh muscle
not all the taste and sip and suckle of mouths
not all the searching and folding
                                        the delving the arching the
sweet   oh, the sweetness of sowing
another baby heart, whose cry they are crying,
will keep them from our moment
that slides, flint-like, between them.

6.
The baby got born.
Life said, good, good.
Carry on! Get her to fifteen,
then let more get born.
But wait, they said, wait a minute.
She deserves more than this.
She's clever, she's beautiful.
Good, good, said Life,
get her to child-bearing age,
get me more of her kind.
But what about her, they cried,
her own slant, her secret glittering grain?

Life shrugged, walked off, the scythe hooked over his shoulder.

7.
Profile to profile
we exchange old thoughts, thought new:
we fear the heartless rain-god, though we can copy and save
everything - artefact, art-work, memory -
everything but time.

8.
In the River that Made the World, they paddled,
the New Ones, hand in hand,
feeling with their toes for the flat cobbles,
the kindlier ones, that led them
on and on through the water's swishing, sunlit
anklets, craning forwards to the moment
shining for them where
the river finds its delta; shining here
inside the bi-valve, sealed
with the thick old-fashioned sticky-tape of fingers -
deep in the flotsam of Ain Sahkri; here.

9.
The stone from which they were cut is part of their embrace
as it was before they kissed, as it will be
after they've kissed again, again
kissing themselves to stone.

10.
But look! Your little lovers,
blunt-headed, froggy-legged -
still together, as if
they had all night to puzzle how to breathe.

Of Those Given to Us to Love

How long it is since some of them were given,
If given's the word. Yet all are competent
To seem, despite geologies of erosion,
  Tenderly recent.

Like chat-room idlers in the timeless given
Of digits, shy of P-to-P flirtation,
They simply like your avatar, don't care
  What's hiding there.

Who didn't want your love when it was given,
Who didn't want a heaven or a token,
Who blamed you for the exit always taken,
  They ought to blush

But queue to be your dream, those old forgiven:
And then, once dreamed, they haunt you. Every day
They cut you up on roads down which you'd driven
  To get away.

Reviews

Angina Days: Selected Poems
Günter Eich, translated by Michael Hofmann
Princeton University Press, £16.95

Apparently
Matthew Caley
Bloodaxe, £8.95

"From the hills on the left bank of the Oder I can look across the river and see the house I was born in, now in Polish hands." So wrote Günter Eich in a poetic 'CV' he compiled in the late 1940s. It's a telling statement, for Eich was, above all, a poet of loss, absence, alienation and endings – an exile in his own country.

In a passage quoted on the cover of this handsome collection, Belle Randall compares Eich to Beckett and Celan as the three post war writers "whose work seems most clearly to answer to Adorno's sense that no poetry can be written after the Holocaust". Or, as Hofmann himself puts it, he was caught up in "the moment of plain speech after the hateful jargon and lying bluster of Nazism."

These are fair judgements. Eich's poetry is pared down until, often, almost nothing remains. There's no bombast, no posturing, no dogma, no ornament; also little joy. But then, what place was there for joy after Auschwitz? He uses adjectives as if he expects them to explode. The results can seem like the literary equivalent of one of those etiolated Modigliani sculptures.

English readers who know Eich are most likely to have come across him through his much anthologised prisoner of war poem, 'Inventory':

> This is my cap
> my coat
> my shaving kit
> in the burlap bag.
>
> This tin can:
> my plate and my cup,
> I scratched my name
> in the soft metal.

Interestingly, Hofmann has chosen not to focus on the years immediately following World War II – there's little from 1948's *Remote Smallholdings,* and not much more from 1955's *Messages from the Rain.* Instead, we're treated to a substantial selection of his later work, from the 1960s and 70s, as well as a welcome choice of poems from his radio plays (Eich was a prolific writer for the radio).

In the late 1940s and 50s, Eich had been a member of Gruppe 47 with the likes of Günter Grass and Heinrich Böll. As Hofmann notes in his valuable introduction, "Eich did exactly what the Gruppe 47 was called into being to do: to cleanse and adjust and simplify the language." As the 50s turned into the 60s, however, and the German economic miracle took shape, his style changed. The taut, frequently rhymed and metrical, lines of the earlier poems start to unwind, sprawl and become more conversational.

The themes, though, if anything become even darker, even more insistent upon expressing a sense of alienation from the world. Many of these poems express a feeling of rootlessness, as in 'Journey': "Pack a bundle, not too heavy / because no one will help you carry it. Sneak out, and leave the door open behind you, / you'll not be back." In others the alienation is even more direct. In 'End of August', he declares:

> There are times I know that God
> is most concerned with the fate of snails.
> He builds them houses. We are not His favourites.

Incidentally, that last line – "Uns aber liebt er nicht" – is perhaps more directly rendered as 'But he doesn't love us': an existential sigh of anguish from a poet who's learned that he has no place in the world. 'Progress' only makes things worse – "Macadamization and death / plan ahead".
As the poems develop Eich seems to become more overtly 'political', as in this from 'Topography of a Better World'

> Vain the cruel hope
> that the screams of the tortured
> might pave the way for a brighter future

or this from 'Dreams', one of his best known radio plays:

> Remember that, following the great destructions
> everyone will provide an alibi for himself to prove he had no part in them.

This play also contains his famous exhortation to "be as sand, not oil in the thirsty machinery of the world!" But I don't believe Eich is primarily a political poet, except in the broadest sense. I think he was motivated by a realisation that the world we've made may no longer have a place for us. It's a prescient message.
Günter Eich is not nearly as well known in the UK as his near contemporary, Paul Celan. Let's hope that Michael Hofmann's assured translation will go some way to correcting that.
Language is just as important to Matthew Caley as it was to Günter Eich, but in a rather different way. Eich felt the weight of each word, in a full understanding of their ability to do harm, measuring out sentences like a starving man rationing rice; Caley gorges himself like a child in a sweetshop.
I don't much like the term 'post-modern'. It was fine when it was limited to architecture, where it designated the magpie-like borrowing of a mixture of styles to decorate what would otherwise have been concrete boxes. Applied to literature it's come to cover so much that it's now practically meaningless. However, I do like one strand of its meaning – the wilful jumbling of high culture with low humour. There's something reassuringly English in the idea that no matter what the situation – death, pain, loss, failure, depression – there's always room for a good *double entendre.* (It also solves Gabriel Josipovici's recent poser – *'Whatever Happened to Modernism'* in England? Answer: it's still here; it's just having a laugh).
In that sense Caley is a post-modern poet *par excellence.* In his pages William B Yeats rubs shoulders with Wile E Coyote; Hoagy Carmichael with Quintilius, Christopher Marlowe and Howard Devoto; Ezra Pound with Clara Bow, Leadbelly, Jesse James and Proust. Just keeping up with all this playful erudition leaves one sweating.
Let's take Pound, for example.

> Apparently Ezra Pound would lay at languorous angles on the inevitable chaise-longue

– feet up, head down – believing as he did
that so prone his seminal fluid would flow from his testicles to his forehead, thus
energising
the brain. He gave new meaning to *"getting laid"*.
('Upside Down')

The poem progressively becomes more intimate, more personal, until "Your ghost stalks the living room, barely wearing a silk sarong, / a swoosh of tinnitus. / Touch my forehead, its cranial swell, I've been upside down for too long". And you suddenly realise it's a love poem. But in order to reach its erotic conclusion, it's taken you from Pound via Gaudier-Brzeska, whiskers and pubic hair, and – best of all – paused to rhyme 'trousers' with 'arouse us'.

Moreover, all this goes on within the confines of a sonnet. Well, sort of. Caley is highly formally creative, using traditional forms but adapting them for his own purposes. There are lots of 'sort-of-sonnets', for example, in which he constructs elaborate structures of rhyme, off-rhyme and eye-rhyme, but allows the metre to wander where it will.

'By the Water Cooler' recalls Auden in its invocation of life happening elsewhere:

Apparently, we gather by the water-cooler
as the city, through blinds, vibrates with drills, ignor-
ing the ploughed-water sound of police launches on the river.

Here he carefully rhymes each line ending, and then gives up after thirteen lines. Many of his best poems, like the fantastic 'Way Out West' sequence, are constructed in a complex 18-line form, in which the first line is (off)-rhymed with the eighteenth and so on. However, it's the sheer verbal ingenuity, not the structures, which will strike you first. Who else could get away with "A Dalmatian happens under. The dots first align, then misalign. / The dog has disappeared"? Or "How oft have I trod this road to find it sky" ('Roadrunner Ode')? Or "'Pudenda,' he says, 'are not on my immediate agenda'," ('Objects')?

The other thing you'll notice is that each poem starts with the word 'apparently'. Well, actually all bar two, and those end with it. It's as if the collection is a pub conversation re-imagined as a renaissance poem sequence.

So, what is Caley up to exactly? I think the clue lies in an introductory quote by Herman Broch: "the melodramatic revulsion which characterises this age as insane, the melodramatic enthusiasm which calls it great, are both justified by the swollen incomprehensibility and illogicality of the events which apparently make up its reality". The world is mad; we have to be a little mad to understand it. People won't get Caley. For my money, though, he's a sixteen carat, dyed in the wool genius. Apparently.

Ross Cogan

De Chirico's Threads
Carol Rumens
Seren, £9.99

Carol Rumens' collection is named after the verse play in the last third of this collection. The play is a fantasy re-telling of the Chirico's development in art, with reference to the ideas that came from the surrealist movement of the early 20th century. It makes good use of soundscape, both in language and accompanying sound effects. Indeed this idea of sound is paramount to how the whole collection hangs together. With appearances by Apollinaire, Andre Breton, the artist's family members, as well as a lost younger sister, the verse play deals with the developing style of De Chirico as he moves through the phases of his career – his later move away from surrealism and how it was then received.

The first third, the smallest, is a sonnet sequence entitled 'Fire and Ice: Sonnets for Late Elizabethan Lovers; a title that may be read many ways. This section beautifully sets out the stall for the rest of the collection, with sonnets that capture a witty suggestiveness beyond the words on the page, such as the dreamscape 'Alba:'

> ... let me dream more and lie late
> Till our fingers melt through the lattice
> Of leaves, and he beckons me onto his office-lounger
> And offers my lips his salad bowl, *prêt-a-manger.*

Behind the poems lies a painterly quality, as in 'De Chirico Paints Ariadne on Naxos,' where the stillness of light spills out from De Chirico's own words, amplified by Rumens' surrounding poem: '*And now the sun has come to a high halt / In the middle of the sky.*'

The longer middle section, 'Itinerary Through a Photograph Album' moves away from the direct weft of De Chirico's 'threads' but there are some shadows at play. 'Count Dracula Creates his Online Profile' is a wonderfully ironic poem dealing with the issues raised by online social networks, blending ideas of class and self-image together to give an unusual mythic archetype.

We can still detect that De Chirico play of light illuminating the background in 'The Solitary Bride.' The narrator of this prose poem is going to meet a lover, "stealing a couple of hours from work." "The white buildings and their shadows" of the journey insinuate themselves almost as another character to the scene of love, which has realist and surreal elements. Rumens avoids the sentimentality trap by matching precise language to equally precise images: "the embrace that's reflected in the mirror," cleverly suggests a stance that hovers between wanting to couple, and be singular.

This disassociation occurs again in 'Diphthongs', a favourite of this reader. The shape of the lines and the long and short white spaces between, contribute to the accruing meaning. This poem documents the process of childbirth, but is more how coping with the abstract element of pain itself, in terms of the vowel based part of the word 'pain', becomes a process (like poetry), a strategy all-absorbing of itself – until the last lines, where the dissociation of mind and body reunify in the reward of life.

'Riddle' could be viewed as an answer to Richard Dawkins' questioning of why poets weren't writing about science in *Breaking the Rainbow.* The poem utilises the strategy of deconstructed lines that emerge from regular, regulated ones to investigate the rainbow and its mythic associations, as how science has dissected:

> we handled you
> phenomenon knifed you open
> somewhereover never-land we dropped you
>
> ...
> all the more wonderful, we said

Yes, even though we write to explain the world to ourselves there is still that aspect that Rumens brings us back to at the end of the poem: "You could still lean down / Iris, and have mercy on the world."

Rumens deserves her accolades included in the cover blurb. She is intimate, restrained and witty, without saccharine or lingual sacrifice, but her view of humanity is harsh: we move through life so fast we scarce have time for it, as the eponymously titled short poem of the middle section shows: "These ports and streets we remember by name – our name, / Yet we never touched their ground, never left the moving vehicle." *De Chirico's Threads* is the light stilled by nostalgia, tempered by hard experience and graft.

Barbara Smith

---

i tulips
Mario Petrucci
Enitharmon, £9.99

If Carol Rumens' *De Chirico's Threads* is a representation of old-school poetry that uses the form as a transparent vessel through which the content and language, is allowed to shine, then Mario Petrucci's *i tulips* is one where form and language become the glassmaker's blowpipe and the product is a new and delicate thing, with much to admire and, yes, surprise and delight.

Petrucci does away with punctuation and capitals, in favour of white space, dashes, splitting words – even syllables – to break lines and stanzas. After a while these effects, added to the momentum of rhythm and good language choice, all conspire to force a fresh reading of poetry in the reader. Alongside this, these elements combine to produce poems quite unlike where one thinks poems should or might go.

His ideas and images loop and hook together like poetic Velcro; each hooks onto the last, but never quite in the way one would imagine. Take 'everyone begins as fish &' which begins with an investigation of the fertilised zygote. Some may be familiar with the idea that up to a point, the developing ovum could be any number of creatures, even a fish or a chick. This initial 'hook' then clutches onto the 'eye' of the narrator's beloved asleep:

upstairs dark

you – on placenta duvet &
hunched round self as wom-
bed ones are?

In turn, this 'eye' connects onto the next 'hook':

– as though

i had just returned from
all eternity to catch you
naked out sleepwalking

space without even
navel-twisted purpled
rope to hold you

So in three steps the reader has moved from the beginnings of cellular life, right through gestation, to the astronaut un-umbilicled in outer space. While this is the surface meaning, the reader must also allow for (amongst many readings) the idea that 'i had just returned from / all eternity to catch you' hints at the idea of the spouse catching the other in the act of *flagrante delicto* – which indeed we all may do in our private dreams.

All of these new associations are made fresh by selecting new word combinations, organising them just so and then trusting all to the hands (and eyes and imagination) of the reader.

Another example of this fizzing energy can be seen in the tying of desire and death together in the poem, 'when you come at.' There may be shades of the idea of the 'little death' experienced at orgasm, from an initial reading of the first part of the poem.

then you steal
in your black-ice
twin of me

slip you
in & stiff me with
what you are brimming

What moves the poem on, out of this realm and into a wider sphere of applicability, is the embodiment in language and white space of the physicality of heightened experience; here translated into words – *playful* words at that:

they push in
the door

through
my hush to find
you there for intent the

content & form the *instead*
of me

Here, Petrucci plays with the image presented and self-references the vessel that holds it: the poem itself, which he just about gets away with.

Another example of this multiplicity of meaning can be seen at the end of 'night entering', a poem seemingly about night, breathing and the small, dark tea-time of the soul where one broods over one's shortcomings is ended thus:

Furied birds

all driven
up beyond you
by this turning in

-ward so towering even
i who made them
must strain

dark for keening.

'Strain' can be read, strain – as in to hear clearly, or strain – as in to sieve the darkness, and here the use of keening is so suggestive that it points the reader not only in the direction of the word keening – to cry, it also encompasses some of its other meanings; sensitive, biting, sharp, acute as well as being very close to the sound of the word 'meaning'.

These poems read like exquisitely made depth-charges of idea/concept/emotion released into a vast ocean with unknown depth. Who knows what targets they will carry up to the surface in the mind of the reader? You can only try it out and see.

Barbara Smith

The Breakfast Machine
Helen Ivory
Bloodaxe £7.95

This is Helen Ivory's third collection. The notes on the back of this book suggest 'There's more than a hint of East European darkness in Helen Ivory's third collection' and, indeed, there is a feeling that the spirit of Baba Yaga may be stalking these pages. Perhaps it is the disturbing chicken in the title poem who *crosses the kitchen/ on squeaky tin legs* or the children's lost teeth that are *all broken and angry,/ chewing at the cold/ metal door to get out.*

The reader is never allowed to get comfortable or complacent; throughout the collection simple, sometimes child-like, images darken and twist in unexpected directions, demonstrating Ivory's truly original imagination. Ivory has a clear narrative voice which, combined with her deceptively simple language, solidly grounds the poems and makes even the wilder leaps of imagination more acceptable to the reader. The poems are populated with characters, and situations, which are strange and often bizarre yet as a reader I feel I can trust Ivory's logic so that the journey through these poems feels somewhat like a dreamscape, where odd conjunctions and unlikely connections seem almost natural.

These poems cut a lot deeper than the currently fashionable quirky; each time a mechanical bird, chicken on tin legs or clever squirrel promises to amuse, the poems slip down darker avenues, driving this reader to tease out the layers of meaning. The squirrel that plays recordings of birdsong with *clever fingers to rewind/ press play /so we can believe in birdsong* is worn down by the futility of pretence until:

His coat weighs heavy on his back,
and if some quick knife
could free him from it, he'd be grateful.
'Birdcage'

A stuffed rabbit breaks away from its mounting and out from a cabinet to trot through the high street amongst such oddities as *a fish with wings* who *played the accordion;* but the rabbit is leading the *newly dead* who are:

following the rabbit in slow procession
towards the freshly built structure of ribs and human hair.
'The Beginning'

A cat *licks/ her babies clean as bone./ Dark red smearing/ the corners of her mouth.* ('Unbidden') and sinister dolls appear in a number of poems, as in 'Jumble Sale' where *a doll with no eyes watches/ from behind the kitchen scales.* Childhood, or childhood imagery, is not a comforting place in Ivory's world and there is a great deal of darkness in the poems but I didn't find them bleak; they are leavened with mischievousness and dry wit, leading me to see them as more in the spirit of loki and puck than the horrors of nightmare.

It would be misleading to suggest that the collection is all strange creatures and mechanical chickens. Ivory's craft together with her assured use of metaphor and reticence has made poems that have been haunting me and drawing me back to read again. In 'Marks', a woman paints her body black and leaves an imprint of herself on linen sheets while '*her lips trace a pattern of wordless shapes/ like the dust left by a moth/ in the palm of a hand*'. Beautifully understated, just the right amount left unsaid and, for this reader, a devastating portrayal of loss. In 'Bedtime Story', a man becomes overwhelmed by the physicality of feelings in his body so that '*he begins to live inside his head/ in the clean-cut world of numbers*'. These are short, simply shaped poems, yet they are suffused with a terrible humanity and seem to teeter on the edge of madness made all the more affecting because of their straightforward language. Ivory's language may be straightforward but it is crafted and precise, each word deliberately placed, increasing the effectiveness of her leaps of imagination.

On the whole, I enjoyed this collection very much for its originality and depth. If I have a criticism, it is that Ivory is just a little too fond of the neat yet mysterious final line. A couple of times I found myself wanting more at the end of the poem while being uncertain whether the poem needed further development or was just too opaque in its ending for this reader. It is not a criticism that will prevent me returning to the collection though, as much of it is of a resonance that unfolds over time, demanding further reading.

Angela France

Whistle
Martin Figura
Arrowhead Press, £10.00

In the interests of full disclosure, I should say that I saw Martin Figura perform the spoken word version of '*Whistle*' at Ledbury Poetry Festival and was spellbound for the whole hour. However, that was several months ago and I have deliberately left the book alone until now so that I may attempt to review it as a collection standing alone.

The poems in *Whistle* tell the story of Figura's childhood, his mother being murdered by his father, and the consequences for Figura and his sisters. This is no 'misery memoir' though; while the narrative arc of the book is clear, he has a light touch and an intriguing focus in the way he approaches painful events. Figura is a professional photographer; photographs, and the language of photography, are used to great effect throughout the collection. In 'Born', Figura suggests himself as a camera from earliest consciousness:

> my first focus
> an iris
> an aperture dilating
> a click
>
> everything is light

while rolled film is used as a powerful metaphor for suppressed emotion

> keep this last film
> dark and tightly rolled,
> hold its tongue
> between your teeth;
>
> *'The boy who'*

Where Figura's photographic experience adds most to the collection, for this reader, is in the way he frames each poem. There is no omniscient narrator, a common device where there is a story to be told: each poem only offers us what is held within the frame formed by the speaker's point of view in that poem. That which lies outside the frame, as with a photograph, is left for the reader to surmise or discover; for instance, the murder happened while the children slept and Figura resists the temptation to elaborate, only showing how oblivious and unaware they were of the dramatic events at the time they took place:

> The ceiling is blank sky,
> the wallpaper a rose garden.
>
> The dressing table's arms are full
> of fallen objects, its mirror dumb.
>
> Through the wall, it causes no more than a ripple
> on the surface of milk.
>
> *'In my Parents' Bedroom'*

The effect of Figura's restraint and framing is to highlight what is *not* said so that the poems appear to be on the periphery, circling and in turn framing the story. Many of the poems are from the point of view of the young Figura so that the sense of them being at the periphery of the main story adds authority because of the way children are often sidelined or hidden away from life-changing events. In this way, the most painful parts of the story are not spelt out but are all the more affecting where they are alluded to or shown in metaphor.

A volcanic shift in his landscape has begun.
He takes to carrying a spoon to tip molten glass
down the nape of his neck and into the gaps
between shirt buttons. Soon this isn't enough
and he wades into its boiling fury.

'Uncle Philip at the Glass Factory'

Figura demonstrates skill and sensitivity in his use of form; throughout the collection, a variety of forms enhance and illuminate the content. In 'Love Letters *(June to Frank 1949-51)*', quotes from his mother's letters are interspersed with short, tight, third person sections of poetry; June's innocence and idealistic view of marriage, highlighted by the more sophisticated language of the poetry sections, is heartbreaking when given the hindsight granted by what follows in the book. In 'Piggotts', the breathless tumble of language in a prose poem invokes the chaotic and loving family of neighbours who rescue the young Figura from a boy's home; and a villanelle insists he '*will be a good boy here*' ('Little Angel') - the form's repetends reflecting both the boy's desperation for the Piggotts to let him stay and the rules he thinks he need to keep.

Whistle covers a great deal of ground, emotionally and temporally; the shifts in time as well as in register are considered and skilfully handled: the sequence showing Frank's retreat into catatonia and his slow recovery being framed by poems in the child's voice seems so natural that the ordering of the poems appears to reflect the way memory works; non-linear with some small peripheral details illuminated and large events skimmed over. This collection is a tremendous achievement; I really hope it receives the notice and acclaim it deserves.

Angela France

Cadillac Temple	**Into the Yell**
Norman Schwenk	*Sarah James*
Parthian Books, £6.95	Circaidy Gregory Press, £6.95

Arriving five years after *'The More Deceived: poems about love and lovers'*, '*Cadillac Temple*' is Norman Schwenk's collection-long musing on the haiku form. This is the haiku as world view: a poet who not only writes haikus, but thinks in haikus. Here however, the haiku doesn't stand as a miniscule and discrete entity, the seventeen syllables or so of its pocket-sized form dwindling-:

'Where the hell is it?'

'Haiku Hello'

Instead, sequences are constructed from haikus, which, sometimes function (or deceptively appear to function) as poems, each haiku being a stanza. Schwenk's preferred use of the haiku sequence however, is to choose say, a season, sense, direction, object, body part (not always something concrete as is proper to the form), and deploy this subject or object as title. The poet then muses (perhaps written over years) in five successive haikus, placed in linear formation. This construct recurs from beginning of collection to end, and at first quick flick through, the lack of formal innovation is almost unappealing. Yes, the sequences are elegant, but once I'd read the collection, something emerged which more than justified the initially repetitive lineation. No matter how much they cascade, no matter the enjambment haiku-to- haiku, these sequences are not poems. But it is the sum total of each haiku sequence which justifies the collection-long form and ultimately, allows this collection to be the most worthwhile (relevant and real) I have read in some time.

> 'I move my body
> against your body calming
> the sad mind-rattle'
>
> *'Bed'*

The formation of sequences such as *'Bed'* allows the stand-alone haiku, the blink of a haiku, to create in unison, a panoramic albeit flash flood sense of image work, which envelops the reader in sustained, but succinct human observation. In this form, Schwenk shows the reader all that we see, all that we know, all we feel, all we want to articulate, but can't ourselves. In Schwenk's attempts to give his reader *everything*, to make sense of *everything* from nipples to car crashes, the poet is perhaps doing what the poet should prioritise and do best: furnish a reader with the opportunity to make sense of *their* world.

> 'they fart in bed now
> is it the end of romance
> or the beginning?'
>
> *'Disgusting'*

Schwenk's preoccupation therefore, is to provide his reader with glimpses, tableau vivante images of our own lives. Small things (the tingle of an un-gloved hand in a bed of nettles, the sexual pleasure in watching a lover eat a portion of chips, a sycamore leaf rotting, a well-earned glass of rosé), are interspersed with the political, the subjectivised, the ideological (the male adult's predicament in wanting to watch children playing, presidents, ownership, wealth etc.). In this way, 'Cadillac Temple' is more than a pleasure to read; it is remedial, a series of truths which Schwenk clicks on and off in our brains- a projector changing slides.

> 'watching the footie
> they never score until you
> go to the toilet'
>
> *'Fan'*

Schwenk deploys the haiku as tease, a peepshow offering snapshots which say to the reader: this is what we know. The haiku then, as Schwenk deploys it, is a quiet space, a location to be solitary in, an observatory from which the poet relates a static image which we can visualise not only because of the filmic and scene-setting possibilities of the haiku, but because Schwenk is adept enough to foreground and explore our most basic similarities as humans, mortality being the most obvious. Perhaps life is a haiku, an observation or experience, then?

> 'were we about six?
> the girl I played doctor with
> is going blind now'
>
> *'See'*

'See' is the sequence which functions most like a poem (in terms of its chronologising and

transference). It is a series of memory-musings on sight, which are particularly fitting to the haiku given its scopophilic propensities. Schwenk's deployment of sight and sense as affirming, connecting, ultimately human, is a trope he shares with poet Sarah James, in her poem *'No Referral'*. In her first collection, '*Into the Yell*', James, like Schwenk, takes note of the small gestures of human existence, for instance, the receiving of ophthalmology results:

> 'I wedge the letter in peripheral vision,
> next to a friend's psychologist card
> and a pile of your unforwarded bills.'
>
> *'No Referral'*, p.33

'*No Referral*' is one of many poems here which make *'Into the Yell'* an assured debut, in which Sarah James works hard to define her writerly concerns as well forge an individual language and voice. Often working inside the first person, James exists within her work, and by that, I mean her voice conjures characters (perhaps just one, perhaps James herself). The poetry then, like a person, becomes cavernous; it contains an origami of imagistic amalgamations, linguistic experimentations and anecdotes shaded by absurd humour:

> 'I penguin-flap past their chopstick legs,
> pinch a single pink feather, unnoticed
> as they're stood wings outstretched,
> preening their perfection.'
>
> '*Pink*', p.24

The journey each poem takes is far reaching, the points of reference extreme. We move from fairytale to pop-culture, to medieval historical, medical, toward the personal, relic object and precious memory. Indeed, the title, '*Into the Yell*', is to do with discursiveness, the extremes and hallucinogenic excess of linguistic expression, but ultimately these poems still manage to be comprehensible and accessible despite their intriguing use of the surreal:

> 'My name is Sarah and I am your guide.'
>
> *'Welcome to the Zoo'*, p.1

The surreal here has much to do with James' other collection-long articulation: dissatisfaction with the humdrum and/or inequality still involved in domesticity, and James does interesting things with the language of the chore:

> 'I scooped dust from melons, swept
> flesh from floors...'
>
> *'The Un-Niceness of Nice'*, p.6

> 'It could take years to
> unclutter this emptiness'
>
> *'For Sale'*, p. 51

Oftentimes, the chore is juxtaposed with myth, folk, fantasy and nonsense, and sometimes, escape toward memory. Indeed, there are many poems in which James explores (or allows us to believe she is exploring) her education, her personal history, her coming of age:

'But what I learnt most as a student
living in the echo of Rouen's l'hôtel de ville,
deciphering my parents' divorce
from a series of late-night phone calls...'
'Studying 'Villains', p.8

These poems are brave. James tackles the modern phenomena of women: emancipated yet implicitly oppressed. *'My Mother's Compact'* (p.41) deliberates on the jarring celebratory mourning of the loss of traditional femininity: *'my compact was gone'*... *'an oyster mourning its pearl'*. Further still, in *'Bitter Pill'* (p.21), the woman is stripped of her entire and expected role, motherhood:

'This is a pill that helps me love my baby.'
'Bitter Pill'

Although I read much of James' assessment of women and their roles as a reflection on current concerns of women rejecting feminism outright, James' debut collection offers her reader an unrepentant articulation of liberated female sexuality: the woman looking at the sex object, in all poems' case, the sex object being the man:

'water corals him'
'6am at the Pool', p.39

There is much in *'Into the Yell'* about coming to terms, a-lot about James' coming to terms. Is this interesting to the reader? Definitely; James makes it so. The hodgepodge of real and un-real, responsibilities and desires, memory and fantastical escapisms do speak pertinently not just about women, but about the way we must live our lives, the way we do live them- through stories, through metaphors, through abstractions and wilful escapisms.

Lucy Tyler

Listings

SUNDAY

First Sunday of each month
Buzzwords
Writing workshop, open mic, guest poet
7pm for the workshop, 8pm for readings
£5/£3 at The Exmouth Arms, Bath Road, Cheltenham. Tel 07855 308122 or email cheltpoetry@yahoo.co.uk

First & Third Sunday of each month
Aromapoetry
Spoken word. Open mic. Free entry. Start time to be determined.
New Venue: Charterhouse Bar, 38 Charterhouse Street, London EC1 0207 608 0858 aroma@x-bout.com, www.x-bout.com

TUESDAY

First Tuesday of each month
Open Mic night,
The Tin Angel, Medieval Spon Street, Coventry, 8pm start.

Third Tuesday of each month
Readings at The Flying Goose
The Flying Goose Cafe,
Chilwell Rd, Beeston,
7.30-9 , £3, including a free glass of wine.
contact: david.belbin@ntu.ac.uk

WEDNESDAY

Every Wednesday
Express Excess: mix of comedy, poetry, storytelling
at The Enterprise, 2 Haverstock Hill (chalk farm tube) Doors: 8.30, show 9pm £5/£3 020 7485 2659 www.expressexcess.co.uk

First Wednesday of each month
Dead Good Poets Society
Doors open 8pm, poetry starts at 8.30pm.
£2/£1 Everyone welcome - each person has five
minutes to perform, and there are a maximum of 24 slots delivered across three sets. Third Wednesday of each month is Guest Night, incliuding short open mic: £3/£2.
Everyman Bistro, Hope Street, Liverpool 1

THURSDAY

Every Thursday
Shortfuse
Spoken word poetry
£5/ £3 8.30 pm (doors) at The Camden Head, Camden Walk, Islington,
London, N1 www.20six.co.uk/shortfuse

First Thursday
Chapter Arts Centre in Cardiff, organised by Seren Books on the first Thursday of the month starting 8.00pm, entry £2.00/£1.00concessions
Each event features readings by two guest poets, followed by an open-mic spot, where members of the audience will be invited to perform their own work.
Information: willatkins@seren-books.com
seren-books.com. 01656 663018

2nd Thursday of each month. 8pm,
Albert Poets
The Albert Hotel
(next to Huddersfield Library)
Victoria Lane,
Huddersfield, HD1 2QF
Contact: albertpoets@live.co.uk

Second Thursday of the month
Ambit:
Readers to be confirmed
£4/£3 6.30pm (doors)/7.30pm (start) at The Bath House Pub, 96 Dean Street, Soho W1 tel:

0208 340 3566
or visit www.ambitmagazine.co.uk

Last Thursday of every month
Dylan Thomas Centre: Last Thursday
A night of readings and song with floor spots for local writers.
£4/£2.80/£1,60 (Swansea PTL & floor performers) 7.30 pm at the Dylan Thomas Centre, Somerset Place, Swansea SA1 1RR
tel: 01792 463980,
visit www.dylanthomas.org or e-mail dylanthomas.lit@swansea.gov.uk

FRIDAY

2nd Friday of every month from Sept – July
Derby Poetry Society
7.30pm at The Friend's Meeting House (room 3)
St Helen's Street, Derby DE1 3GY
Guest speakers. Meeting fee: Visitors £2.00; Members/Students 50p
For programme of events contact:
Maria Fox on 01773 825125 or
mariafox56@aol.com
Gina Clark on 01773 825215

3rd Friday of the month,
The Poets' Cafe
South Street Art Centre,
South Street
Reading
8pm for 8.30pm £6/4 cons.
listing: www.readingarts.com/southstreet
contact: afh@afharrold.co.uk

WORKSHOPS AND COURSES

Salmon Creative Writing Workshops
Salmon Publishing run regular weekend creative writing workshops at the Salmon premises: Knockeven, Cliffs of Moher, Co. Clare. These include all aspects of writing and publishing. The facilitator is Salmon's director, Jessie Lendennie, who has conducted workshops all over Ireland and the U.S., for many years.
Numbers are limited to 7 per weekend.
Sessions will run two weekends per month.
For more information, or to book, email salpub@iol.ie or telephone 065 81941
Salmon Publishing Website:
http://www.salmonpoetry.com/

COMPETITIONS

Ware Poets Opening Poetry Competition 2011
Closing date: 30th April 2011
Sole Judge: Carole Satyamurti
For poems of up to 50 lines
First Prize £500. Sonnet Prize

For further details send SAE to:
The Secretary
Ware Poets Open Poetry Competition 2011
Clothall End House
California
Baldock
Herts. SG7 6NU
or download our entry form from
http://www.poetrypf.co.uk/images/compware2011.pdf

The Poetry London Compeition 2011
Deadline: 1st June 2011
The Poetry London Competition 2011 is now open for entries. This year the judge will be the acclaimed English poet Paul Farley.

First Prize £1000
Second Prize £500
Third Prize £200
plus publication in Poetry London
Four commendations will be awarded £75 each
Entries must be in English, your own unaided work, and not a translation of another poet.
Entries must not have been previously published, in print or online.
The maximum length is 80 lines.

Entry fee is £3 per poem for Poetry London subscribers, for non-subscribers £5.

For competition rules and to download entry form, see www.poetrylondon.co.uk

Poetry Contributors
in order of appearance

Mike Barlow won the National Poetry Competition in 2006. His first collection *Living on the Difference* (Smiths Doorstop 2003) was short-listed for the Jerwood Aldeburgh Prize for best first collection. His second collection is *Another Place* (Salt 2007). His pamphlet *Amicable Numbers* was a winner in the Templar Pamphlet Competition 2008 and a Poetry Book Society Pamphlet Choice.

Maitreyabandhu has won the Keats-Shelley Prize, The Basil Bunting Award, the Geoffrey Dearmer Prize and the Ledbury Poetry Festival Competition. He lives and works in the London Buddhist Centre and has been ordained into the Triratna Buddhist Order for 20 years. He has written two books on Buddhism.

Abegail Morley's collection *How to Pour Madness into a Teacup* was shortlisted for the Forward Prize Best First Collection (2010). Her work appears in a number of anthologies, and magazines such as the *Financial Times, Frogmore Papers, Other Poetry* and *The Spectator*. She is guest poetry editor at *The New Writer.*

Howard Wright was runner up in Poetry London Prize, 2009; shortlisted for 2010 Torquay Prize and Bridport Prize. His collection *King of Country* was shortlisted for the 2010 London Festival Fringe New Poetry Award. He lectures in the University of Ulster and recent poems have appeared in *The Shop, The Penniless Press* and *Staple*.

Robin Houghton lives in East Sussex and is an internet marketer and copywriter. Since joining the Brighton Stanza last year she has been writing more seriously and recently had her first poem published in *The Rialto.*

David Troupes is a Massachusetts native now living in West Yorkshire, where he works in social housing. His first collection of poems, *Parsimony*, is available from Two Ravens Press, and his graphic art can be perused online at www.buttercupfestival.com.

Colin Will lives in Dunbar. He has served on the Boards of the Scottish Poetry Library and StAnza. His fifth collection, *The Floor Show At the Mad Yak Café*, was published by Red Squirrel Scotland in 2010. His publishing house, Calder Wood Press, specialises in poetry chapbooks.

Suzannah Evans lives in Leeds and travels on foot. She is studying for an MA in Writing at Sheffield Hallam University and has had poems published in magazines including *The Rialto* and *Brittle Star*. She is poetry editor for *Cadaverine*, an online magazine for under-25s.

Robert Etty lives in Lincolnshire. His work has appeared in a range of magazines, including *The North, The Rialto, Poetry Review, The Frogmore Papers* and Smiths Knoll. His most recent collections are *Half a Field's Distance: New and Selected Poems* (Shoestring Press) and *The Horncastle Executioner* (Nunny Books).

David Clarke lives in Cheltenham. He has had poems published in *Popshot, Blart* and *Words Myth*, with further work in upcoming issues of *Staple* and *Ellipsis*.

Rachel Spence is a writer and journalist based in Venice, Italy. Primarily she works as an art critic for the *Financial Times*. During the late 1990s, she had poems published in *The New Writer* and won an award from Poetry Life magazine. After a break of several years, she began writing poetry regularly again in the summer of 2010.

David Starkey is the Poet Laureate of Santa Barbara and Director of the Creative Writing Program at Santa Barbara City College. His most recent full-length collection of poetry is *A Few Things You Should Know about the Weasel* (Biblioasis, 2010).

Steve Sawyer's passion for poetry and the stage began at an early age. Before completing an M.A. in creative writing at Manchester University he had already worked amongst other things as an actor, stand-up comic and most recently, as a university lecturer in philosophy and the social sciences. Steve, who now lives in Sheffield, is a performance poet whose work reflects his humour and his strong ties with the north of England where he was born.

Pam Brough lives on a hill farm near Flash. Her work includes theatre, poetry, residencies/writing in the community and radio, with occasional Arts Council grants, most recently for *Jinglebones,* a long narrative poem. Other work includes *The Burma Play,* an on-going production supported by The Co-operative.

Jonathan Taylor is author of the memoir *Take Me Home* (Granta Books, 2007). He is Senior Lecturer in Creative Writing at De Montfort University and co-director of arts organisation and small publisher Crystal Clear Creators (www.crystalclearcreators.org.uk)

Julia Fairlie lives in West Cork, Ireland, and is a freelance copyeditor and proofreader. In some of her previous lives she was a bookseller, hospital cleaner, typesetter, microelectronics technician, psychiatric nurse, and played fiddle in a ceilidh band. A few of her poems and stories have appeared here and there.

David Holliday was born and educated in London, but has since settled in Chesterfield where he sings in and occasionally conducts the local Male Voice Choir, and formerly edited *Scrip* and *iota* poetry magazines.

Daniel Barrow's poetry and short fiction has been published in *Horizon Review*, *Spilt Milk* and the anthology *Vertigo of the Modern*. He has written on music, books, film, TV and art for *Plan B, Horizon Review, Muso* and *The Boar*, and is currently writing a book on English radicalism and cultural memory for Zero Books.

Julia Stothard lives in Middlesex and is a member of Sunbury Poetry Society. Her poems have appeared in *Iota, Interpreter's House, Weyfarers* and *Pulsar Webzine*.

Richie McCaffery was born in Newcastle in 1986. He is the recipient of a Scottish Arts Trust bursary in honour of Edwin Morgan and his poems have been accepted by *Stand, Magma, Envoi, Other Poetry* and *The Interpreter's House.*

Nicola Warwick was born in Kent and now lives and works in Suffolk. She has had work in various magazines including *The Rialto, Magma* and *The South*, as well as commendations and prizes in competitions.

Vidyan Ravinthiran's poems have been published widely, in journals which include *Poetry Review, The Times Literary Supplement, Magma, The North* and *Poetry Wales*. He is anthologised in *Joining Music With Reason* and the forthcoming *Salt Book of Younger Poets*. A pamphlet, *At Home or Nowhere*, was published by Tall-Lighthouse Press in 2008.

Martin Mooney has published three collections of poetry—*Grub* (Blackstaff, 1993), *Rasputin and his Children* (Blackwater 2000, republished by Lagan Press, 2003), and *Blue Lamp Disco* (Lagan Press, 2003). A fourth collection, *The Resurrection of the Body at Killysuggen*, is due from Lagan in 2011.